To Lauren,
Many blessings,
Marissa
11/10/18

Carried

A Pilgrim's Story

MARISSA ZAMORA

WESTBOW
P R E S S®
A DIVISION OF THOMAS NELSON
& ZONDERVAN

This book is a work of non-fiction. Unless otherwise noted, the author
and the publisher make no explicit guarantees as to the accuracy of
the information contained in this book and in some cases, names of
people and places have been altered to protect their privacy.

Scripture taken from the New King James Version®. Copyright © 1982
by Thomas Nelson. Used by permission. All rights reserved.

WestBow Press books may be ordered through booksellers or by contacting:

WestBow Press
A Division of Thomas Nelson & Zondervan
1663 Liberty Drive
Bloomington, IN 47403
www.westbowpress.com
1 (866) 928-1240

Because of the dynamic nature of the Internet, any web addresses or
links contained in this book may have changed since publication and
may no longer be valid. The views expressed in this work are solely those
of the author and do not necessarily reflect the views of the publisher,
and the publisher hereby disclaims any responsibility for them.

Any people depicted in stock imagery provided by Getty Images are
models, and such images are being used for illustrative purposes only.
Certain stock imagery © Getty Images.

ISBN: 978-1-9736-3968-8 (sc)
ISBN: 978-1-9736-3970-1 (hc)
ISBN: 978-1-9736-3969-5 (e)

Library of Congress Control Number: 2018910981

Print information available on the last page.

WestBow Press rev. date: 09/20/2018

To my dear father,
Florentino Zamora Jr.,
who walks beside me
every day of my life.

My purpose dwells upon those who aren't sure,
in hopes these simple words
may ignite a complicated thought
that maybe ... just maybe.

CONTENTS

PART I

The Making of a Pilgrim

CHAPTER 1

Don't Ever Stop Learning

My son, if you accept my words and store up my commands within you, turning your ear to wisdom and applying your heart to understanding.

—Proverbs 2:1–2

I always loved school. It was easy and a form of entertainment for me. As a child, I thought it was fun. Recess was even better. I can't imagine my life without an education. I love learning. I love the excitement when something in my brain just clicks and I get it. For every problem, there is more than one solution. Figuring those answers out was just cool.

After graduating high school in 1978, I enrolled at Victoria Junior College to start working on my basics and eventually got into nursing school. I had graduated cum laude from Victoria High School and walked across the stage at our awards assemble at least three or four times to receive scholarships and awards. It helped me jump-start my education, which I had to acquire on my own since I had left home a few months before. I was surprised every time the emcee called my name. It was totally unexpected. My dad made it to watch me receive these awards, and I would have given anything to have found him in the crowd. Unfortunately, he had to return to work, and we never connected on that special day, but at least I know he was there for me. Better yet, I know I made him proud.

Although I was working a couple of jobs—one at the nursing home and another at the Playhouse Cinema—I was still going to school full-time. My problem was that it was like I was a little bird that had just been released from its cage, and my focus was not on school. It was on life and learning about all it had to offer. My grades suffered greatly, mainly because of no sleep and no studying; I rapidly deteriorated academically.

I did get into nursing school, but the first year, I lost a week due to an unexpected surgery. The following year, I had to start over, and unfortunately, the second year, I lost another week because of my father's passing. I couldn't catch up; my mind was foggy. My focus was not on school, and I found myself on scholastic probation.

The next couple of years were lost. I wouldn't have given them up though. I learned a lot about life, about struggling, laughter, friendship, betrayal, partying, and survival—the lessons that school does not teach you. It was that time in life when you're entering adulthood but just not quite ready to grow up. What an adventure.

With the birth of my firstborn, Nikki, life slapped me right between the eyes and said, "Okay, it's time. Now you have to be responsible for someone else's life." That's when education made its second attempt to get my head straight.

I enrolled at Pan American University in Edinburg, Texas. It later became part of the University of Texas, but it was still Pan Am the entire time I was there. At first, I did get into the nursing program, but then I really wanted to try other interesting subjects, such as teaching and art. I took so many classes in the arts field and thought it would be lovely if I could be an art teacher.

Throwing pottery on the wheel was a passion. Creating jewelry, designing, and drawing were just fun. The problem was I was being challenged creatively but not academically. I needed to feed on critical thinking, and I missed the nursing aspect of caring for people. I knew deep inside I was born to be a nurse.

The Soul of Nursing

The heart will start the chain reaction,
the soul will follow without retraction.
It's a heart that is filled with a passion for giving,
with respect for the dying and love for the living.
A tender touch will abolish the pain
and paint a rainbow to banish the rain.
When demands seem so great, a merciful mind
will comfort the victims of misfortune unkind.
It's the light in the darkness, a radiant flame
that devours the hurt and spoils the shame.
Solemnize the bloom of the heaven-sent seed,
acknowledging it is the taker's need.
Prepare for the clowns and leave them with scorn.
Nurses cannot be made; nurses are born.

Coming to terms with the fact that I needed to get back into what I was meant to be, I decided to get into LVN school instead. Nikki had come along, and taking care of her was my priority. I figured I could get my LVN degree in a year and then work in the nursing field while I was earning my associate degree. I did just that. But I had to make a decision. The night before I started the program and for the next year, I would stay focused and not allow anything to steer me away from my education. I had to continue working to support us, and I did so as a cocktail waitress, because the hours worked well with school and I was taking a decent salary home. I really hustled my tables to make as much as I possibly could.

I worked in a very nice lounge at the Sheraton in McAllen while putting myself through school. One day, the general manager called me to his office. I had never been called to the office before, so I was really nervous. I knew who he was, as he often came through the lounge to check that things were running smoothly. As I walked to his office, I kept trying to think of what kind of trouble I was in.

He caught me off guard when he asked, "Exactly what are you doing? How are you working so differently than everybody else?"

I was completely lost. I had no idea what he was talking about. "What do you mean, sir?"

He continued. "I mean, how in the world are you outselling every other waitress that works with you? Not by two or three times but by five times! For every hundred dollars one waitress sells, you sell five hundred! How in the world are you doing that? You get the same number of tables, no more hours than anybody else, but it's like you're nonstop. I want everybody to sell like you, so tell me what you're doing."

I was dumbfounded! I had never paid much attention to how anybody else was working. I just did my job.

"Well, sir, I hustle. I'm here for a purpose. If you stay on top of your tables, don't let anyone go dry, memorize every single drink so that your customer doesn't even have to tell you every time and anticipate needs, then you'll get taken care of by the customer. You, sir, only pay me $2.25 an hour. I have to depend on my customers to take care of me, so I take exceptional care of them."

I just told my boss that I hustled. Oh heaven forbid! I hope he understood my explanation. This job was helping me get through school, but it was up to me to get the most out of my job. I didn't have any secrets to give away. I think he knew that.

I wouldn't have given up my year in LVN school for anything! I learned so much in such a short period of time that it was unbelievable. My instructors had their fingers in my face, and boy, I had to know the answer every time they asked me a question! Every drug, every diagnosis, every problem had better have a solution.

My particular class started with thirty-six students back in 1986. Amazingly, twelve of us made it through. That was the toughest year of my life. I was the only student in our class who worked. Everyone else had a spouse supporting them or lived with their parents. I had a spouse, but I was the financially responsible one. Not one weekend was spent having any kind of fun. The entire year was spent caring for Nikki and getting my homework done. I was rewarded for my determination by graduating valedictorian with a 4.0 GPA! I couldn't believe it: from scholastic probation to valedictorian. Who would have thought?

As soon as I graduated, I got my first licensed job at the hospital where we did our rotations. I eventually left my waitressing position. It was ironic. I went from making an average of fifteen dollars an hour to help people kill themselves with alcohol to $5.75 an hour to save their lives. Yes, I took a deep cut in pay, but the service I was providing meant more to me than anything. I knew in the future it would pay off, and with the graciousness of my dear Lord Jesus, he led me in the right direction, into the career I was meant for.

While in LVN school, I encountered a situation with one of my instructors that stuck with me for the rest of my career. We were learning about how to give an enema, and she beat into our skulls that we should *never* use an IV pole to hang the bag on while instilling the enema. She said it was absolutely imperative that we hold the bag in our hand so that we could raise and lower it, thereby controlling the rate and even stopping the flow by holding it level. That made sense to me, but I also noticed that the tubing had a roller clamp, and she didn't tell us anything about using it. Apparently, they didn't have roller clamps when she went to school in the Dark Ages. It made common sense to me that I could use the clamp to control the rate. So I went about doing exactly what she told us not to do. I hung the bag on the IV pole while I gave my make-believe patient their enema. When she saw me doing that, she came stomping across the lab floor right up to me with a raised voice.

"Why are you hanging the bag when I specifically told you not to?" she scolded me.

I responded, "Because if I use the roller clamp, I can control the rate and use my other hand to hold the tubing in place. It's just much easier."

She was speechless and realized that just because you learn something a certain way in school doesn't mean there aren't other ways of doing it. As I've mentioned, for every problem, there is always more than one solution.

The following day, she pulled me aside and told me that she appreciated me challenging her. I taught her something. In the meantime, I also learned something new about myself. Don't be afraid to challenge your instructors. If you're wrong, that's what they are there for. If you're right, then both of you are learning.

Because I paid for my education, I challenged my instructors in my mind every single time I walked into their class. I secretly whispered, "Okay, sir/ma'am, I'm getting ready to pay you for one hour of your time. You better not let me walk out of this classroom without teaching me something I don't already know." Don't ever walk out of class without learning something new. Remember, you're paying for it.

A much more serious lesson was to be learned from my statistics instructor. By now I was working on my BSN degree years later, and statistics was a prerequisite. This was by far the most rewarding and challenging class I took in all my educational years. I stayed up late to study, sometimes until one or two o'clock in the morning, if needed, just to stay on top of this class. I was working full-time at the hospital, so my schedule was toilsome. I kept an A average and worked hard to stay there. We had to do a long-term project during the entire semester and complete it close to finals. Just as the end of the semester was approaching, the instructor informed us that if we earned an A on the long-term project, we wouldn't have to take the final. I was ecstatic! I knew my project was a winner, as it had to do with data collection regarding documentation at the hospital, and I was just so proud of my work and eager to impress my instructor. I had so much confidence that I had aced my paper that I decided to give my brain a break and stop studying for the final. I was so elated that I wasn't going to have to take it. I even considered publishing my work because it was that detailed.

On the day she handed back our projects, my smile instantly vanished when I saw a B+ on the top of the page. The first thought that crossed my mind was the fact that I was going to have to stay awake for the entire week to catch up on the stuff I was supposed to be learning for the final. I was in shock. I couldn't even breathe. *Oh dear Lord, forgive me. What have I done?* I had to fight the tears of self-pity. *What in the world am I going to do?* I was so angry with myself until my instructor called me to her desk after she gave the class a brief period to review their project scores. She informed me that I had done two things wrong on my calculations, and she would give me an opportunity to find and correct them. I scurried back to my desk and eagerly got to work. I searched and pondered. I tried one thing, then another. When I finally thought I may have found the solutions, I returned to her desk with project in hand. I prayed. She reviewed my papers, and after a minute or two, she scribbled over the B+ grade and changed it to an A. My prayers had been answered. We reviewed the issues, and I thanked her kindly for teaching more than she knew. This one incident was by far the most valuable thing I learned in all my years of schooling. I learned to never stop learning—one of the most valuable lessons in life.

You don't have to go to school and earn a degree to be educated. There are many people in this world who don't have a degree and are extremely intelligent, wise, knowledgeable, and smart. Being well-read can get you there. Being street-smart is wise as well when it comes to survival. There are many forms of education, but the one common thread is to never stop learning.

CHAPTER 2

The Magic of Paddle Wheel Drive

Now I plead to you brethren, by the name of our Lord
Jesus Christ, that you all speak the same thing and that
there be no divisions among you, but that you perfectly
joined together in the same mind and in the same
judgment.

—1 Corinthians 1:10

Paddle Wheel Drive was the perfect cul-de-sac to raise my children.
Nothing more than hard work and determination got us there—
two major ingredients for success. We were the fourth house on the
street to be built in the early nineties. I'll never forget at the end
of moving, sitting in the garage exhausted from constant lifting,
pushing, pulling, bending, and walking. One of my new neighbors,
Theresa, walked into the garage with a six-pack of Dr. Pepper. She
introduced herself and welcomed us to the neighborhood. That was
such a good sign that we had made the right move. She was kind
and offered to help, but we had just finished the last few boxes, and
I said, "I think I just want to die here!"

Oh the hours of grueling overtime it took for me to gather the funds necessary for the down payment to get us into this new home. I had never invested in such a huge undertaking, but this was the American dream, owning your own home. At thirty-two years of age, I finally made it to the place where I could raise my children and build their future. Just as any average mother, their safety, well-being, and happiness were my priority. New memories were soon to begin, along with a large segment of my adult life to be spent in our lovely new home. Paddle Wheel was ideal, and I thanked my good Lord for leading us to it.

Somehow my driveway became the ideal Halloween hotspot. I loved decorating my front yard for different holidays. For Halloween, I would put out a cemetery with funny sayings like, "Here lies Jonathon Blake, stepped on the gas instead of the brake," just really silly stuff. I had a huge blow-up horse-drawn hearse with a skeleton that would rise and fall from his coffin inside the hearse. I even made an eight-foot Frankenstein that was absolutely adorable. Yes, an *adorable* Frankenstein. All of these were made out of plywood that I drew, cut, and painted myself, except the hearse of course. I put tables out on the driveway, and that's where I had all the goodies—candies, cookies, cupcakes, for the kids, plus Jell-O shots for the adults. My neighbors would join me, and we hung out on my driveway visiting. Most everyone would pass out their candy there, so it was a one-stop shop for the entire circle. Kids loved it, and so did the adults. The problem was that the kids were getting upset that I would not let them have a Jell-O shot. To solve this problem, the following years, I made virgin ones as well so that everyone could have them. That was just fine and dandy until one year I got the two mixed up by accident. I noticed several of the kids kept coming back for more. And then it hit me—oh heaven forbid! The kids had been grabbing the wrong color of Jell-O shots! I felt so bad, but everyone got a kick out of it. From then on, I decided the kids would always have red, and all the other colors would be for adults only. No wonder everyone liked hanging out on my driveway for Halloween.

For approximately eleven or twelve years, I organized a Christmas block party. I absolutely love Disney and probably meet the criteria of being a fanatic. It all started back around 1995. I had drawn, cut, and painted a life-size Snow White and the seven dwarfs. I am not an artist, but Disney has these "learn how to draw" books, so I just followed those instructions and blew them up to the size I needed. I also made candy canes and outlined my front yard with them, draped in little white Christmas lights. I received so many compliments from my neighbors. My best friend, Lisa, who lived right across the street, asked me to make her a set for the following year. Then she went a step further and said, "Wouldn't it be great if everyone on the street had a different scene and we outlined the entire street with candy canes?" I envisioned the scenes and loved her brilliant idea, so it was a go for the following year. I had no idea how much work it was going to be.

We held a candy cane workshop the following April, and most of the neighbors participated. Paddle Wheel Drive only had thirteen houses. Everyone picked their favorite Disney movie, and I worked all year to make it happen. They provided the materials, and I provided the labor. This woodworking became my passion. Although time-consuming, I loved doing it. At the entrance to Paddle Wheel, in the very first front yard, I made a huge sign that read "Welcome to Paddle Wheel's A Christmas With Disney." In the center of the cul-de-sac, I decorated it with a Precious Moments nativity scene. It's simply not Christmas without Christ. I made angels and several characters surrounding our Lord Jesus in his manger. He is the reason for the season! Needless to say, our street became very popular during the holidays. Lines of cars would drive their kids through very slowly, admiring all the characters and lights. I learned that some families would play games, slowly driving down our street to see who could name the most characters. Doing something that makes a child smile is so fulfilling to the heart.

We all started decorating our yards right after Thanksgiving. About two weeks before Christmas, we would block off the circle to traffic, and I, the neighborhood leader, would take charge and organize the entire block party. Neighbors would pitch in and arrange, decorate, or bring tables and chairs, participating in any way they could. Everyone brought a finger food or something to nibble on. We got members of the high school band or choir to come and sing Christmas carols, which served as a fundraiser for their summer camp. I put out a huge multi-gallon container of hot chocolate. The best part was, regardless of his busy schedule, Santa always found time to pay our party a visit. I would go to the local Dollar Store and purchase thirty to forty one-dollar, age-appropriate toys, ranging from three to twelve years of age, and he would pass them out to all the kids. He would also hand out candy canes. We always had enough to go around, and whatever gifts I had left I would save for the following year. Upon Santa's arrival, the kids would form a line and anxiously wait for their turn to sit on his lap and tell him what they wanted for Christmas. The parents would take memorable pictures. This was by far better than any mall experience with Santa and so much more personable. The line was shorter, and it didn't cost anything. I was so fortunate to have such wonderful neighbors for the longest time there in Katy. Thank you, Lord, for such blessings.

CHAPTER 3

An Aunt Minnie Inspiration

A wise man is strong, Yes, a man of knowledge increases strength. So shall the knowledge of wisdom be to your soul; If you have found it, there is a 'prospect, And your hope will not be cut off.

—Proverbs 24:5 and 24:14

"Auntie Week" was an awesome creation. Katy, Texas, is a suburb of Houston. My wonderful, loving sister, Thelma, and my little (not so little) brother, Aaron, live in Austin, where my mom also resides. My niece, Nina, and four nephews, Ronnie, Ricky, Roman, and Jordan, rarely spent time with my kids, Nikki, Gina, and Laura. Like most families, we only spent time together during holidays, graduations, weddings, and funerals. The cousins never got a chance to spend quality time with each other like I did when I was a kid. Therefore, I came up with a brilliant idea based on my childhood memories, which my aunt Minnie inspired.

As a child, I grew up in Farmington, New Mexico, just south of the Colorado border, from the time I was four until I was fourteen.

We were the only ones who had moved out of South Texas (Rio Grande Valley), so we never got to visit our extended family except during the summers. My parents would drive us down there, dump us with my grandma, and leave us there for the three months of summer. I loved it. This was the time we got to spend with all of our cousins, and there were lots of them! I loved them all. We would play outside the majority of the time. At night, my grandmother would put blankets out in the front yard, and we would tell scary stories, catch fireflies and put them in glass jars, and play silly tag games. The Catholic church was right across the street from my grandma's house, and we would go climb the ledge that encircled the church. We would pretend we were mountain climbing and do our best not to fall off the make-believe cliff. The priest and the nuns never chased us away. They let us play on the church and the premises as if it were our playground. That doesn't happen anymore, I'm sure.

My Aunt Minnie was in her twenties at the time. She was single, lived with my grandma, and had an awesome job. She worked at the bank, and I seriously thought she was rich. It was only common sense to the young and naïve that anyone who works at a bank must be rich, as they are surrounded by money. Right? She would come home for lunch faithfully every day at the same time, and my grandma would have lunch ready for her. We would run to Pete's, the corner store, and buy her a Coke, back when it was the "real thing." Being that my aunt was single, she was the one who spent time with me and my siblings, taking us places and doing fun things like going to the beach. She created so many fond memories for me. She was truly my inspiration. I wanted to be that Aunt Minnie in my niece and nephews' lives. She is the reason I created Auntie Week.

It's so funny when I think back now how I would do anything to get her attention. There were so many of us that there just wasn't enough of Aunt Minnie to go around. I was always jealous of my brothers and my cousin Baby because she would spend the most time with them. My father also favored Aunt Minnie because she was just so adventurous. I wanted so much to be like her. She taught me the importance of making happy memories with the ones you love, with the little time you have on this earth. I think every family should have an Aunt Minnie.

Time

(Dedicated to my Tia Minnie)

Embrace the here and capture now; forever I will steal,
Your simple touch is the spark that's everlasting real.
Magic fills the room with the cracking of your smile,
I'll throw away reality to keep you for a while.

They say it's a matter of time but time does not matter,
For give to me this simple choice and I shall choose the latter.

Embedded in my heart your love will always be,
Happiness is taking flight with each new memory.
You leave imprinted in my soul, in my heart and song
What life is truly all about, the ride that we are on.

They say it's a matter of time but time does not matter,
Use it wisely while you can therefore I'll choose the latter.

As I drift into my slumber, into my vibrant dreams,
We'll meet at heaven's pearly gates and come up with a scheme
To make the angels laugh and play much like we used to do.
And just like here, it shall be there,
The smiles because of you.
                                                    I love you Tia.

Auntie Week lasted one full week each summer. I would pick up the kids and create a fun-filled agenda for every single day. It would be timed and calculated, and it would have purpose, including educational, but mostly it would be fun, fun, fun. I had to inform my brother and sister that they were not invited. At first, they were a little hurt, but once they understood my reasoning, they got over it. This was my quality time, as well as the cousins' quality time together. They loved the idea and made every effort to get the kids' schedules adjusted so that this special week could take place. It lasted five years until it got to the point that the kids had so much going on in their busy lives that they couldn't give me that full, uninterrupted week. I would include a sports event every year, an Astros game, which of course was the highlight of the week. Fishing was a very important item on the agenda, and I saw to it that they got an opportunity to fish at least once during that special week. An educational activity also ensued, such as museums, NASA, and the firehouse tour.

During one Auntie Week, I made the kids watch the movie *The Pianist*. After the movie, I gave a ten-question test, which they were made aware of before the movie (so that they would pay attention!). The individual who scored the highest would win twenty dollars. Nina won. Although she's not mine, I believe Nina is a mini-me. I love her so very much. The next day, we had lunch at Schlotzsky's, followed by a visit to the Holocaust Museum. They were able to correlate many items in the museum to the movie, which helped deepen their understanding. We even got into one of the boxcars they had seen in the movie. It was at that point I sensed some emotions taking place, including my own. It was a great learning experience, and I know so because a few months later, Sylvia, my sister-in-law, shared a story with me. Roman, her son and my youngest nephew, told her that his fourth-grade teacher asked the entire class a question regarding the Holocaust. Roman enthusiastically raised his hand.

"I know, I know!" Roman cried out.

He answered her correctly, and then she asked another question. Again he raised his hand.

"I know, I know!" said Roman, and again he got it right.

After the third question, with no one else raising their hand, there went Roman again, with a huge smile. Naturally, he knew the answer.

She finally asked him, "Roman, how in the world do you know all of this?"

His response, "Because of Auntie Week!" Best story ever.

As far as fishing was concerned, I drove them once to Galveston, and the other years it was Port Aransas. The first time in Galveston, I learned a valuable lesson regarding tags. The kids didn't need a license due to their ages, and I knew nothing regarding fishing licenses. Come to find out, all the kids were catching these beautiful, huge bull reds! When I found out they couldn't keep them, I was livid. Why didn't anyone tell me? I certainly didn't know to ask either. So the deckhand explained it to me thoroughly. "No, the kids didn't need a license, but if you want to keep your bull red, you can only if you tag it." Therefore, other passengers on the boat were asked if anyone wanted to tag my kids' bull reds. Oh, I was so upset. Believe me, I learned quickly. I would never make that mistake again. They did catch a bunch of small sharks that we got to keep, and the educational portion of this activity was that they had to learn how to fillet their own fish. My fabulous neighbors at the time, Steve and Kathleen, participated in teaching us the technique. Naturally, Nina showed us all up and did the best at filleting her sharks. We filleted and fried them and had an incredible fish dinner, poolside in my resort-like backyard. That was Aunt Sylvia's description. I spent an incredible amount of time building our backyard to give my kids that vacation feel.

I would prepare a timed agenda and share it with them every day so that they would be prepared. Most days started at 7:00 or 7:30 a.m. because breakfast needed to be taken care of prior to taking off, and I liked to leave by eight. Poor kids, they got a taste of what obsessive-compulsive behavior really is! They probably felt like they were still in school during their summer vacation! Oh well, it was Auntie Week; we had things to do, places to see, and people to meet along the way! I kept them fully engaged and entertained with all kinds of activities, including pool tournaments, Bunco, card games, water volleyball, family board games, and movies. I even took them to the horse races and taught them how to gamble. Of course, that fell under the educational section for that week. I believe that was one of their favorite activities. The most important goal of Auntie Week was to create happy memories. I believe I was quite successful in that endeavor, as evidenced by the kids still talking about it years later. Give a child a material gift, and a year later they will forgot what you got them. Give them a happy memory, and they will remember it forever. This was one of my favorite accomplishments in raising my children. Just like my aunt taught me, life should be all about creating happy memories with the ones you love.

CHAPTER 4

The Right Thing

Be sober, be vigilant; because your adversary the devil walks about like a roaring lion, seeking whom he may devour. Resist him, steadfast in the faith, knowing that the same sufferings are experienced by your brotherhood in the world.

—Peter 5:8–9

God bless unions. Unions are a good remedy for organizations and employers who don't treat their employees fairly or take care of them like they should. When you don't have the tools you need to do your job or are made to work overtime without getting compensated, and you've tried to the best of your ability to improve or correct poor working conditions, then by all means, consider joining a union. So yes, they may be needed in some situations, but I passionately believe my profession isn't one of them. Nurses are educated people, fully capable of improving their working conditions and environment without having to pay an outside source who doesn't even know anything about nursing. Not one organizer was a nurse.

Through no fault of my own, somehow I took the lead on educating nurses about the opposing views of unionization. I found myself developing a team to fight against unionizing at my facility, one of the first private hospitals in the state of Texas to be unionized. The first election, we lost by eight votes, a thin margin. We filed charges for unfairness of the election based on all the negative experiences my team and I encountered. I had been denied a request for a room so that my team could educate the nurses at our hospital. The union, on the other hand, was granted a room, and they offered all kinds of goodies to get the staff to come down. They were reeling in nurses who didn't take the time to educate themselves before making an incredibly important decision. Good food and statements such as "We can get you a lot more money for a lot less work" seemed to work well with lots of staff. I'm a firm believer in "If it sounds too good to be true, it probably is." I didn't fall for that scheme, but I was curious as to why they were at my facility. Who invited them? Who was complaining? I had always felt I was working at one of the best hospitals. Administration was so supportive, morale was fantastic, teamwork was phenomenal, and we were a great hospital, so why had these people shown up? I approached my manager and asked her a question regarding the union.

"I can't answer that," she replied.

"Why?" I asked.

"Because we are not allowed to talk about the union."

"What?" I couldn't believe my ears! That made no sense to me. My only resources, my supervisors, had a gag order placed upon them. *Oh my, this is so wrong. This is dreadfully wrong.* I started talking to my peers, and there were several who felt the same way I did. *Something is terribly wrong with this picture, and we're not getting any answers. So here I go, Google, teach me.* Within the next few weeks, we created a strong team to fight the uninvited union that was blindsiding the gullible nurses. We met on a weekly basis at a nearby restaurant because the hospital wouldn't let us have a room. At first, they did grant my room request, but then I later found out the union threatened the administrators with a part of their "Neutrality Agreement" that stated if they assisted an individual or group of individuals that went against the union, they would press unfair labor practice charges. Therefore, our room request was denied. There were so many things wrong with this scenario.

After the election and the arbitrator siding with the union, in August 2009, I pressed federal charges against the union and my employer with the help of my awesome lawyer. I didn't tell a soul. Everyone found out because it made it into the *Houston Chronicle* on that August morning. When I got to work the morning it was published, my boss called me to her office.

I closed the door, and she said to me, "What are you doing?"

I replied, "The right thing."

My little wonderful hospital had been placed on the map, and somehow I became the leader of the anti-union movement. That was certainly not my intent. My focus was not trying to get nurses to be anti-union. My goal was to encourage nurses to educate themselves, to evaluate the pros and the cons prior to selling their signature, before making such a critically important decision. I simply wanted to make sure all nurses got the education they needed in order to make an informed decision. Regardless of my intent, I was still labeled as anti-union. I was fine with that. I found myself traveling all over Texas, speaking to small and large groups of nurses, trying to educate them on the negative impact that unions had on our profession. No one else was doing it, and someone had to.

Unions promote themselves by presenting all the benefits they have to offer. That is understandable and expected. They are a business; they should do that. I actually thank the good Lord that unions came into existence many decades ago. I clearly see through history how desperately they were needed. We have laws in place such as forty-hour work weeks and elimination of child labor because of their great service. They promoted many good labor laws still in place today. Once companies and business changed their treatment of employees to more positive ones, the need for unions deteriorated. It's unfortunate that once they attained a taste of power, they have never been able to let it go.

The problem I was experiencing was the lack of knowledge about or exposure to the negative impact they had on our profession. I used the analogy of a car dealership. You go to buy a car, and the car dealer only tells you about how wonderful it is, about all the positive reviews it has received, the incredible engine, and the latest, greatest style, and you purchase this vehicle based only on that information. You don't go on a test drive or ask any questions. Then you take it home, only to discover it gets fourteen miles to the gallon, it doesn't have power steering, and it shakes if you go over forty miles per hour. Then you find out the insurance is outrageous because of the engine size, and you had no idea what you were getting yourself into, but it's too late, because you already signed.

Deciding to bring a union into your facility is no different. It's a major decision that requires knowing both sides of the issue. Being fully informed is critical, and that is what I was trying to stress. Be educated. Be informed. It's simple. It's the right thing.

I believe that you should choose nursing because you care about people, but unfortunately, sometimes people become nurses because of a dollar sign. Believe me—a patient knows immediately which one of those nurses is taking care of them.

In January 2011, I found myself sitting on a four-member panel, giving testimony in front of a congressional committee in Washington, DC. I testified on my experience with the union and the negative impact I felt it was making on our profession. I sat with Steve Forbes, of Forbes 500, and the Honorable Elaine Chao, who served as Secretary of Labor the entire eight years of the Bush Administration. She was stunningly beautiful, and when my lawyer informed me she was married to Mitch McConnell, Majority Leader of the Senate, I was bewildered. I was told they were a powerhouse in this little world we call Washington. I met many people, and at one point I looked around and felt so awkward and out of place. I was in the midst of all these political elites in their $500 suits and shiny shoes, and I was there in my little black Walmart outfit. When I came back from all that silliness, I felt so much more secure in my own being. Sometimes when you try to do the right thing, you find yourself in situations where you take a step back and absorb everything that has happened, and you ask yourself, "How did I get here?" I felt like I was a no one who temporarily stepped into a someone world. I'm glad I did because I felt in my heart that it was definitely the right thing to do.

It was quite an experience, and I was so fortunate to have been given the opportunity to voice my experience and opinion while politically important people actually listened. It became even more memorable after the hearing, when I went to visit the Library of Congress and the Supreme Court buildings, while my lawyer, Glenn, graciously served as my tour guide. Utterly amazing and such spectacular sites. I am very proud to be an American. God has blessed America.

To this day, I still totally disagree with the unionization in my profession, although I respect every nurse's right to make their own decision. On the other hand, I just can't help but feel sorry for all those nurses who are handing over some of their hard-earned money to a business that is probably not doing much for them. Of course, if it's doing something great and worthwhile for them, then that's a good thing. My philosophy is that as long as you're getting what you're paying for, then I'm okay with that. More than likely though, most nurses are not. And they don't have any idea how to get out of it.

The charges of my lawsuit were resolved a couple years later. One of the charges that stood firm was the fact that a facility cannot deny the same privileges, such as providing a room, for any group that wants to educate on the opposing side of unionization. As far as the other charges, the court did not see anything illegal, and therefore they were dropped. I still made a positive impact on the pursuit of education, and that is all that matters. Thank you, Lord.

CHAPTER 5

My Island, My World

And let us not grow weary while doing good, for in due
season we shall reap if we do not lose heart.

—Galatians 6:9

Jim doubted me. One of many. This jolly-looking gentle clown,
with his crooked smile, absolutely doubted me. He owned one of
the condos above mine, on a fifteen-mile stretch of island along the
Texas Gulf Coast, known as Mustang Island. Mustang Island Beach
Club (MIBC) had become home just the year before. It kind of felt
like a private society due to its quaint size and very few residents
that reside year-round. I was one of the lucky five owners who called
MIBC home. Five out of thirty-two units, as the rest were year-
round rentals. I bumped into him in the stairwell.

"So I hear you're going on a hike," stated Jim.

I responded with a gleaming smile, "Why, yes. Yes, I am, and
I'm preparing every chance I get."

"Well, maybe twenty-five years ago it wouldn't have been such
a crazy idea, but at our age, honey, I'd think twice if I were you,"
he said.

"Ha!" I replied with an *I'll show you* attitude. "You obviously don't know this woman very well. When I set my mind to do something, Jim, I don't stop till it's done. I don't give up easily."

That pretty much sums up my perseverance in a nutshell. Sometimes when people doubt me, it fuels my desire to try even harder to accomplish whatever they are doubting about me. I'm not sure if it's those who doubt that I want to prove wrong or if it's just me I'm trying to prove myself to. Perhaps both.

Finding my way back to Mustang Island took a while. A long while. My children believe that was my midlife crisis, wanting to be on the beach or just close to the water. I wanted both, but even more so, I wanted to learn how to become a really good fisherman, just like my dad.

I had visited the island a few times before but never paid it much attention. Once when I was eighteen during Senior Skip-out day, I went with my high school sweetheart. That year, the school administrators had eliminated the special day when they allowed seniors to dress up; it was causing too much distraction, and they felt it was inappropriate. We seniors, being as rebellious as we were back in the seventies, created our own senior celebration: Senior Skip-out day. It worked out beautifully. The majority of us met on the island, had it counted against us, and still managed to walk across the stage at graduation.

Another time when I was about twenty, I went with an Iranian friend of mine. It was the early 1980s during the Iranian Hostage Crisis. He was just a student, and a pilot for that matter, and needed friends during this time. I became one of them. I don't remember much of those young and dumb years, but I do recall sitting in the passenger's side of my car when suddenly the police officer's flashlight was shining in my face. I felt like I was on stage. I froze. Such a bizarre experience. I remember waking up around noon, lying on the powder-fine sand, burnt like a lobster, surrounded by hundreds of beachgoers. Where did they all come from? I'm so fortunate those experiences were few and far in between. Lord, I was a young sinner, and I graciously thank you for forgiving me and my misguided decision-making.

I found my way back when my husband at the time lived in Port Aransas for about a year for work-related purposes. It was during those frequent visits that I began appreciating the island much more, but it never crossed my mind that I would someday call it home. I took all the kids during Auntie Week for our fishing excursion on my cousin Jorge's boat. He took us out bay fishing for the day. Fishing is an extraordinary sport and teaches numerous skills, including patience and appreciation, especially when you get to reap the rewards of devouring your own catch. Port Aransas and Mustang Island could not have been more perfect.

Sandcastles

Sandcastles
And
Dreams
Can
Arrange
Subtle
Thoughts
Leaving
Emptiness
Scattered.

CHAPTER 6

I Could Hear the Water Calling Me

In all things showing yourself to be a pattern of good works; in doctrine showing integrity, reverence, incorruptibility. Sound speech that cannot be condemned, that one who is an opponent may be ashamed, having nothing evil to say of you.

—Titus 2:7–8

It was sometime in my mid-forties when I felt a strong call to the water. I dreamed of living right on it. I imagined waking up in the morning and walking out on my deck, sitting in a comfortable chair and watching the spectacular sunrise creeping onto the water's edge as the rolling waves tickled the sand. Sipping on something, anything—it didn't matter. I just wanted to be by the water. That was a dream, and I wanted to get close to that vision, as close as I possibly could. I knew that in order to make this fantasy a reality, it was going to take a lot of hard work and super-long hours. So the next couple of years, I worked an abundance of overtime, putting away every penny I could save. Toward the end, I was working full-time at the hospital and three days a week at an oncologist's office, running her six-chair infusion suite. I adored Dr. Iqbal and learned so much from her. I would start IVs or access lines, give chemo, draw blood, run labs, just do it all, and I absolutely loved it!

During this savings time, I would drive down to the coast on my one day off and just go look, go survey, go search for that ideal spot. I started driving down Crystal Beach, north of the popular city of Galveston. I had visited this pleasant community before. The same awesome neighbors, Steve and Kat, who taught us how to fillet the fish had a fun-filled family week on that beach every summer. Since I was considered part of their family, I was naturally invited. This was their way of creating happy memories with their family, and I was so fortunate to be a small part of it. Unfortunately, every time I visited this beach, the water was a nasty, angry brown. The waves were always mad, and the water's horizon hid the washing machine down below. I just didn't feel it. I wasn't getting that vibe I was looking for, so it was simply a no. It's a good thing I didn't invest a great deal of time there because it would soon be wiped out by Hurricane Ike, leaving one house standing. What an incredible picture Mother Nature had painted.

I continued traveling a few miles at a time with my allotted time off from work, looking for that ideal beach retreat. I usually traveled alone, as my children had better things to do with their weekends. I slowly followed the curve of the Texas coast and visited towns like Surfside, Matagorda, Fulton, and Rockport. I even started looking at condos for sale in the South Padre Island area, but after about a zillion views of nothing impressive, I eliminated South Padre Island. It's such a popular section of the Gulf Coast, probably the most visited, but I shied away because I was born in the Rio Grande Valley and spent many years watching the island develop. I remember back in the early sixties, my parents would drive us across a small, narrow, extremely long, and very straight bridge. It was never-ending. By the time we got on the island, there was only one visible structure. This isolated structure provided shade for several picnic tables. That was it, nothing else. Now, it's a different world out there. It's really nice, yes indeed. The high-rise hotels, all the bars and restaurants, the gift shops, it's gorgeous and all, but there was a questionable nag that I couldn't shrug off, telling me South Padre Island wasn't for me. I didn't like that during every weekend and especially on holidays, an influx of people infested the island, and the condition the beach would be left in was far from admirable. I simply cannot stand litter. I didn't want to have tolerate a non-caring attitude toward our environment. It appears the town has taken care of that issue, but back when I was shopping around, it was still a problem. On top of all that, I felt the condos were well overpriced. I knew my budget and was comparing costs all along the coast.

For two years, I had been working, saving, and searching for a condo on the Gulf so that I could learn how to fish, so I could relax on the sand and take long peaceful walks on the beach. By now it was June 2011. I took my daughter Gina Christine, my middle child with severe middle-child syndrome, with me to go explore the Corpus Christi area and the beaches they had to offer. Apparently, she didn't have plans that weekend, so she decided to tag along. We stayed at the Best Western on North Padre Island. Gina was my little party animal, focused on having fun and living a happy-go-lucky life. She obviously inherited all my party genes, while Nikki, my oldest, secured all my mommy genes for herself. We arrived in the evening, went and enjoyed a lovely dinner, and had a few drinks during a pleasant conversation about what the future may hold. With just a bit of a tipsy feeling, we walked across the street to the nearest bar. Driving is simply not an option if you ever have more than one. There were only four girls at the bar, an obvious bachelorette party with their silly hats and giggly conversations. I was feeling confident enough to locate some courage, and without much of an audience, I attempted my first-ever karaoke to one of my favorite songs, "Mr. Jones" by Counting Crows. I royally ruined it, as expected.

I remember my father once telling me, "Mija (which means *my daughter* in Spanish), there's nothing in this world you can't do ... except sing."

He was so right. There is absolutely nothing in this world I cannot do ... except sing. And I'm okay with that. I am so okay with that.

I was only nineteen when my dad died. It had only been a year since I had left home. I was very close to my father; he was absolutely the biggest and most positive figure in my life. I would visit him at his car pool meeting spot when they arrived from Edna, which was where he worked with the Bureau of Reclamation as a civil engineer. We would meet at least two or three times a week in secrecy. It's sad but, that was the hand that we were dealt, and we weren't going to let anything keep us apart. Perhaps it was his passion for fishing that soaked into my blood, and that was why I could hear the water calling me.

If Heaven Had a Telephone
(1979)

If heaven had a telephone I'd call you every day,

I know the Lord would answer and this is what I'd say...

"Hello Lord, how are you? I hope you're doing fine. I know you must be busy so I won't take too much time. First I'd like to thank you for watching over me, but even more important, watching over my family. Lord, there's someone special, I'd like to say hello, If my Daddy's not too busy, could you call him to the phone?"

I'd hear the Good Lord giggle, surrounded by his grace

He'd say "Yes my child," with a smile on his face.

He'd call my Daddy over, he'd say "Just had to check, but since she's been a good girl, I let her call collect."

Then I would hear my Daddy, he'd make my whole world bright,

To hear "How's my princess doing?" is my ultimate delight!

"Oh Daddy how I love you and how I miss you so, for something in my heart tells me that you know."

We'd chat for just a while, so much we had to say. I let my Daddy know, indeed he made my day.

Then we'd hear the operator, time suddenly flew,

"Try to make it short so other lines can get through."

My eyes would become swollen, I couldn't help but cry

When me and my Daddy said our sweet good-byes.

I talk to you in my prayers so I won't feel all alone.

Just want to let you know I'd call … if heaven had a phone.

CHAPTER 7

God's Holy Water

The earth is the Lord's and all its fullness, the world and
those who dwell therein. For he has founded it upon the
seas, And established it upon the waters.

—Psalm 24:1–2

I will never forget the experience I encountered the following
morning. This was truly unforgettable. We found our way to
Mustang Island, took a left, and a few miles later we saw a sign that
read Beach Access 3, so we took it. Upon approaching the scene,
my eyes began to widen. *Oh my heavenly Lord, this can only be your
creation. It is so celestial it almost doesn't look real.* After passing
the dunes, a serene, magical beach opened up, and I found myself
stunned and speechless. My eyes were wide open, absorbing his
gracious beauty. *Oh my heavenly Father, this is it. My prayers have
been answered! I don't know where I'm at, but this is it.* I started
running toward the beautiful, peaceful, gentle blue waves that rolled
onto a mirror-like receding water line, passively stroking the leveled
sand that seemed miles long. It was an image beyond belief. The
sand made me feel like I was walking on clouds. It gave me such an
angelic feeing.

I yelled at Gina, "Mija, this is it! This is the beach! This is the one I've been looking for! I have to live here!"

She replied, "Yes! Mom, this is incredible. I love it!"

That's when I looked around and didn't see any houses. There were not even any structures down this beach access. I thought, *Okay, that's okay, I'll just live nearby. I will find a place very close to this beach. At last I found my beach!* My heart was so full of joy that after two years I had finally found my beach. Now the real work was to begin, finding a nice but affordable place.

The first real estate agent I worked with wasted about four months of my time, not to mention the money I threw away. I know it had a lot to do with my limited budget, but she just wasn't fulfilling my wants and visions I had for residing by the water. She was Russian with a strong, mesmerizing accent. I remained with her for that length of time because I wanted to give her the benefit of the doubt. After several months, I finally gave up on her and went with an angel God apparently sent my way to solve all my condo-search problems. Dana, my condo angel, made it happen within a couple of weeks. I was astounded! She took me to look at a few available units at MIBC, some requiring lots of work and others well above my financial abilities. They were all so cute, so perfect, but the one I fell in love with was beyond my limited funds. Dana had faith though. She was the specialist and knew far better than I did. She could make magic happen unbeknownst to me, as I only visualized disappointment after what I had already been through. I was down, just a little depressed for a very short, until Dana made a statement that gave me hope. Most of God's angels make magic, and indeed she did.

She said, "Don't give up. There's no harm in trying. Let me negotiate, and let's see what happens."

After a few days of negotiating, Dana did make it happen. She got them to come down by $11K. Almost there but not quite. To get closer to my number, I asked her to make one final negotiation on my behalf. Would they consider reducing it by $2K more if they took all the furniture? It was old, used, and needed upgrades anyway. Plus, I had my own furniture. It would save me even more money not having to purchase a storage room to put all my furniture in, so it was definitely a win-win situation for me.

"Yes." It was a yes! I did it! After almost two and a half years, my little midlife crisis dream was finally becoming a reality. I love you, Dana. I love you, Jesus!

Onward

drifting slowly onward
     to a place I've never been,
  leaving all the good things
       and a game I couldn't win.

looking toward tomorrow,
     not knowing what is there,
  waking up each morning,
       living with that fear.

plans to go on searching
     for all the things I love,
  looking at my yesterday
       has never been enough.

the echoes of my music
     and the softness of my song,
  standing way behind me
       to know I was not wrong.

friends and dreams beside me
     help me play the game and win,
  and I'm drifting slowly onward
       to a place I've never been.

CHAPTER 8

Staying Focused

Blessed is the man who endures temptation; for when he
has been approved, he will receive the crown of life which
the Lord has promised to those who love him.

—James 1:12

Right after I found my condo on the island, I purchased it in
November 2011. Now I had to come to terms with how to deal
with my home of the past twenty years. I had worked so hard to
make it memorable for my children. It turned out to be such a
great entertainment zone for my girls and their friends. We were
garage people; that was the local hangout. I had decided our home
on Paddle Wheel was becoming more of a burden because it was
so high maintenance and I was the only one taking care of it. The
electric bill was outrageous in the summer. The taxes and insurance
were more than I wanted to handle. All the girls had moved out,
and I didn't want to spend the rest of my life pulling weeds, cleaning
the pool, and maintaining everything. It took a while to come to
the conclusion that even though this was where I wanted to die, I
didn't want to die exhausted. Therefore, it only made sense to me
to move into my condo, which was supposed to just be a vacation

home, until I could find a more suitable place to reside. The initial plan was not to make my vacation home a primary residence, but the idea certainly didn't hurt.

Prior to putting the house on the market, I did a complete makeover to about 80 percent of our home. The way I had designed the backyard was truly like a resort. I had designed islands of palm trees and plants surrounding the pool, and the fence line was speckled with plants and statues that I was quite proud of. As far as the interior of the house went, I painted every single room and got the entire kitchen upgraded. It was beautiful. My bestie, Lisa, was a real estate agent, and there was no question of whom I was going to list with. After her assessment, she gave me a ballpark figure of where I should start and where I should settle. I didn't doubt her assessment, but I did know that the passion that I had put into creating this home was more than money could buy. I bet everyone feels that way about their first home. I told her she was crazy and that we wouldn't list for less than $20K above her figures.

She laughed and said, "Okay, now who's crazy?"

The housing market was at an all-time low, but I was in no hurry to sell. This is where the funny part comes in. We opened the house to the market on a Thursday morning, and by Thursday afternoon, I had my first viewer walk into my home.

When she walked into the entryway, her mouth dropped open, and she said, "Yes! Oh goodness yes, this is it!"

My first thought was, *Wait— wait a minute. You just walked in. You haven't even seen it yet. You're barely in the living room.*

She kept on saying "Wow, wow, wow." Every step was a bewildered "Wow!" I really think she was bit overdramatic. My home was nice but not extravagant beyond imagination, which is how she was portraying it. By the time she made it outside to my backyard, she had her husband on the phone, informing him he had to come as soon as he got off work. She didn't want to take any chance of someone coming to see my home and having competition. I remember when she walked into the garage, she made a statement.

"Can you just leave this exactly like it is?"

I laughed but appreciated her sincerity. We barely negotiated over the next six days, and when they realized we were not going to budge below my so-called crazy amount, they said yes. This is what really bewilders my mind. They purchased it with cash! Do you realize how much faster that happens? This meant I needed to move out, and I needed to move out fast!

> You shall love the Lord your God with all your heart
> and with all your soul, and with all your strength.
> —Deuteronomy 6:5

I had been employed at one of my favorite hospitals for the past eight years and absolutely enjoyed my time there. I had informed my supervisor that I had been looking for a place on the beach, so they were well aware of my future plans. After I purchased my condo, I informed them I would be turning in my notice. Before I could even write my notice, I was summoned to the Chief Nurse Executive's office. I adored that lady! Patti and I had worked together for several years at another facility in Houston, and we had a pretty tight professional relationship. After a lengthy conversation, she convinced me to stay on a few more months to help train the next manager for the unit I had been working on. I had been the assistant manager for the past year and had a lovely schedule, Monday through Thursday, ten-hour days, with three-day weekends. All that with no pager! I loved it immensely but would give it up to go live by the water. Patti informed me that I could keep my same schedule and commute to the island on the weekends. She would help me find a place to stay, as she knew I now had no home in Katy. I told her that finding a place to stay would not be a problem, as I knew my incredibly sweet neighbors, Steve and Kat, would let my silly self stay with them. They loved me as I did them. Due to the high level of my commitment to my employer, I stayed on just as they requested. I didn't mind commuting to the island and faithfully did so for the next three months.

By January 2012, I started looking online for what was available in Corpus Christi. The first job that I applied for, I was hired. I think I blew away the Assistant Administrator and Director who interviewed me when I told them about my involvement with the nurses' union. I was also interviewed by three charge nurses, Wayne, Susan and Tandy, who worked on the unit I was applying for. That interview was the toughest one of all. These three charge nurses grilled me. The one named Tandy, even stood up and slammed a book on the floor, yelling while telling a story. I questioned myself, *Am I applying for the right job?* I continued with the interview, but I had to be very careful with their questions regarding unionization. They could not participate in the union because their roles fell under the management umbrella, but they certainly had a lot to say about it. I didn't want that to disqualify me, so I kept it under my breath. I didn't want them to know immediately that I had a target on my back.

CHAPTER 9

Be Thy Servant's Servant

For you brethren, have been called to liberty; only do not
use liberty as an opportunity for the flesh, but through
love serve one another.

—Galatians 5:13

One of the places I had traveled to back in 2009–2010 to educate
nurses was a hospital in Corpus. Little did I know that two years
later I would be employed by these people! I started as the nurse
manager on a cardiac unit. It was a twenty-five-bed unit focused
on cardiac patients but took overflow of practically everything.
Yes, even gynecology cases. I was an unknown, and no one knew
my management style. Needless to say, during the first few months
I was getting acclimated, I was not well liked at all. And that was
okay. I was there to do a job, and it simply got done. I was not
authoritative, but if it's a rule, you simply follow it. If it's your
job, you simply do it. It was simple. My management style was
simple. Many misinterpreted my style as authoritative or that of a
dictatorship, but it wasn't. I believe in shared governance. Everyone's
opinions and ideas matter. My door was always open. I made every
effort to be visible on the floor as well. I would even go in on the

night shift and spend time with them. It took months upon months for them to start realizing I cared about them as individuals, not just employees. I cared about their work/life balance. I spent close to $1,000 just bringing them goodies, doughnuts, kolaches, cookies, and more. I cared about how they felt about their jobs, that they felt appreciated and valued. That mattered to me. It took a year, and I had an extremely difficult time hanging on to make it to a year.

Two things were making me extremely unhappy. One, I could not fix the process of replacing a nurse, once they left, in a timely manner. And when it came down to it, I was expected to be the fill-in on the floor. Oh, don't get me wrong. That is my passion. I absolutely love bedside nursing and have mastered it with great pride. But the problem is in today's health care world, we are invaded by technology, and you must know how to run and navigate each and every computer program necessary to accomplish and document your work. Oh my heavens! I'm so computer illiterate it's shameful. I am intimidated by them. Because of this, I was terrified every time I had to go take care of patients. Even just medicating a patient for pain, it would take me ten to fifteen minutes because the program required fifty to sixty clicks of the mouse. I was so uncomfortable having to ask my staff how to print a consent because that was a different program. Figuring out how to reconcile their discharge med list was painful for me. I needed to do all of this every day to become comfortable. I know I'm a good nurse, but not knowing the computer sent me home feeling like I was the worst nurse ever. I couldn't live with that feeling. *I'm above this. It' broken.* Therefore, after that first year, I decided I had to fix it.

I approached my boss, Jason, and informed him of my decision. I told him that he needed to allow me a couple of years on the floor to get comfortable with everything that was expected of my staff. I needed to master and be able to function in all the roles that reported to me. I needed to be able to function as a charge nurse, a primary care nurse, a nurse assistant, a monitor tech, and even as a secretary if I was ever going to be successful in the nurse manager role. Reluctantly, he understood where I was coming from and granted my request. God is so good. Everything happens for a reason.

Just so happens that when I brought my case to his attention, he brought to my attention that the hospital was looking for a few CPOE (computerized provider order entry) Super-Users. I wasn't sure what that meant. Well, come to find out, because of Obamacare, all hospitals were required to become 100 percent computerized by 2015. Mind you, in January 2013, I was going through a divorce and in the midst of a major career shift. When I informed my children that I had been offered a position that required me to learn a program and then teach it to hundreds of people, they unanimously voted, "No!"

"No, Mom, don't do it. You'll make a total fool of yourself," both Nikki and Gina agreed.

"You don't know computers, Mom. It's not a good idea," they further stated. Well, all their negativity upset me. I thought, *Wait a minute. Maybe God is opening a door for me that's offering me an opportunity to not just learn how to work with a new computer program but master it!* Just to prove them wrong, I took the job. But I also took it because I wanted to challenge myself and become comfortable enough to do all those jobs listed earlier. I informed my boss I would accept this temporary "Master Trainer" position but that I wanted to return to the floor once it was completed, which originally was supposed to be March through August 2013.

A total of five of us nurses were hired into these temporary positions, and just as my children had predicted, I felt totally out of place. I was at least twenty to thirty years older than all of them, and I had no computer training other than the programs my boss had taught me in order to do my job. I was so uncomfortable with what I had gotten myself into, but I wasn't going to let it beat me. I took the study materials home, and after I got off work, I would study for hours. I remember traveling out of town one weekend to Houston for training, and I had to utilize every minute on the road to study. I studied hard. I grasped more and more each day.

When we started training nurses in the classroom, I would occasionally make a mistake, and I could feel the eyes roll like I was a complete idiot. I didn't let that bother me. I was dedicated to my role and was going to give 110 percent of myself no matter what. Once you commit yourself to a job or role you are fulfilling, do it to the very best of your ability. Be positive, be open, absorb everything you possibly can, and grow. Don't ever stop learning. Yes, you will make mistakes, we all do, but learn from them and move on. I believe that it is because of my work ethic and work philosophy, instilled in me by my father, that I was the one who the director of the CPOE program asked to stay just a little bit longer, as he needed support to run this new department until it was established.

I was proud of myself, proud that I had proved my children wrong about their mother. Proud to have learned this enormous program and become more computer literate. Proud because this opportunity exposed my name and who I was in the organization. I wasn't just another nurse anymore. Doctors now recognized me, and my administrators did as well. They made me feel greatly appreciated for playing a role in our total electronic conversion.

I hung on a little longer while the other four master trainers returned to their former positions. A couple of them were offered new positions. I was asked to stay until sometime in October 2013. My boss was getting irritated that I had not returned, and he had to make a decision to allow me to return or submit a request to replace me. I elected to return to my former unit as a primary care nurse and relief charge nurse.

I had become friends with several of the other master trainers, one who eventually became my boss. She was so young and sweet. She called me one day and asked to speak to me regarding my former position, Nurse Manager of 4-Tele. She was taking it into consideration and wanted my advice. I asked her to come over to my condo, and we would visit. When she came, I gave her the full-blown truth of it all. The ups and downs, the pros and cons, and all its reality. Yes, it was challenging but could be rewarding. I told her it was a golden opportunity to help her grow and develop her career. I also promised her I would make sure she was successful. I would become one of her core charge nurses and be readily available for support or advice. I adored that girl.

She introduced me to Sharkathon, a surf-fishing tournament they hold once a year on North Padre Island National Seashore. She approached me in December of that year and asked me if I would be interested in taking a hike on the Camino-de-Santiago in Spain. She said that she and her boyfriend were thinking about doing it and asked if I'd be interested. I thought about how exciting it would be and asked her to give me more information. I would think about it.

CHAPTER 10

Birthing a Major Adventure

There are many plans in a man's heart, nevertheless the
Lord's counsel that will stand.
—Proverbs 19:21

I had no idea Jesus was involved. I had no idea it was all about one
of his disciples, St. James. I started doing my research, and the more
I learned about it, the more mesmerized and intrigued I became.
Different sources had different theories, but all in all, it was basically
the same story. After Jesus's resurrection, he appeared before his
disciples and gave each of them specific instructions on where and
how to carry on the Word of the Lord. St. James was given the
responsibility of spreading the Gospel of Jesus into and across the
great nation of Spain. For the next forty-four years, he did just that.
Upon establishing the Christian religion in the Iberian Peninsula
(now known as Galicia), he returned to Judaea on a pilgrimage and
was beheaded by King Herod Agrippa. He is known to be the first
disciple that was martyred.

Then he killed James the brother of John with the sword.
—Acts 12:2

It is also known that the scallop shell is the most recognized symbol of all pilgrims on the Camino because it is found on the shores of the peninsula. It was also used as a secret arrow during the Moorish conquest when Christians were being robbed, raped, and murdered on the trails. These shells helped the pilgrims find their way to the cathedral.

How St. James ended up in Santiago is also surrounded by many theories. My favorite was that his remains were placed in a stone coffin and sent out to sea. Legend has it that angels guided his coffin around the nation of Spain from the Mediterranean and north into the Atlantic before making landfall at Patron on the Galician coast. Apparently, two disciples met the stone boat that, by the way, didn't have any oars, sails, or sailors. They took St. James's body and eventually buried him in current-day Santiago de Compostela. Around AD 813, a hermit by the name of Pelayo had a dream in which a star shined on a nearby field. After finding that field and several days of digging, he discovered the coffin. He reported his findings to the church leaders, and once the leaders concluded it was indeed the remains of St. James, they built a great cathedral on that very spot in his honor.

As Christians learned of the discovery, they began walking from their homes to the church to pay homage to the Saint and then walked back to their homes. Thousands upon thousands of pilgrims walked to the cathedral for this very purpose, and eventually these trails began forming. The trails made it easier for the next generation of pilgrims to find their way. Again, the scallop shell played a major role in pilgrims finding their way.

During the Muslim rule of Spain, the number of pilgrims diminished greatly due to the trials and tribulations experienced by many Christians. Regardless of the turmoil, many were adamant about paying homage to the Saint, so they began different routes, one of them being the Northern Route.

The more I read, the more passionately in love I became with the story of this great disciple and the development of these trails. I decided I absolutely had to do this hike. For the next eight months, this adventure would be my focus. I worked overtime to save all the money I would need to invest and the money I would need to get there and live off of for a month. I continued to do all my research and investigate all the *Caminos*, their differences and similarities. I quickly decided I would take the Northern Route simply because of the water but also because nothing is more beautiful than seeing God's creative artwork where land and sea caress. It was common sense to me to take the more physically challenging route, regardless of my age, mostly because I wanted to see it for myself on the other side of this beautiful and magical world.

I prepared physically by taking numerous hikes around my home, all over Texas, and even one in Colorado. The first hike I took was from my doorstep down the boardwalk to the beach. I walked down the beach from MIBC to the next closest island, which was twelve and a half miles one way. I started at 7:00 a.m. with approximately seven to eight pounds in my backpack, which included about two pounds of water in the bladder. I really enjoyed that hike, as I absolutely love my island. I found sand dollars, and unusual seashells, occasionally enjoying the waves on my feet and digging my toes in the sand. I climbed over the jetties and took a break at the state park. It was fun. It only took me four and a half hours to make it to the popular Padre Island Burger Company on the northern tip of North Padre Island. I met my sweet and very supportive boyfriend, Jay, and my daughter Gina there for lunch. They had passed me by as I was walking over the Packery Channel Bridge and yelled to me, asking what I wanted them to order for me. I responded, "A bacon cheeseburger with jalapeños," and within ten minutes, I was sitting at the bar with them, chowing down on that fabulous burger. I had been dieting in preparation for the Camino, so this was a major splurge, but I needed the calories to make it back, and besides, I had already earned it! After an hour break, I headed back down the road and the beach and made it back to my condo by 5:00 p.m. I was so impressed with myself—my first twenty-five-mile hike, and I did it in nine hours. I felt confident that I could absolutely do this.

> For we are His workmanship, created in Christ Jesus
> for good works, which God prepared beforehand so
> that we would walk in them.
>
> —Ephesians 2:10

This was just the beginning. I completed eight months of preparation for the adventure of a lifetime. I don't remember exactly when Jamie, my boss, informed me that she and now her fiancé had to back out, as she was moving to Houston where he resided and therefore would not be able to go. I didn't think even for a second of canceling this trip. I was going even if it meant I had to go by myself. It's so peculiar how things work out, as I learned later. A pilgrimage is so much more when it's just you and God. So again, my initial motivation was the adventure and the history of these trails that I found so intriguing, and I was going to accomplish this challenge if it was the last step I took.

I continued prepping with day-long hikes, one of which was from my condo to the barn. I had purchased an acre of property after my pastor at the time preached on investments.

I'll never forget his statement, "If you want to invest, invest in what God made. You will never go wrong."

Common sense tells you that land was one of those items. Therefore, I bought an acre, purchased a metal building, and had it constructed on my new property at first for storage but also a place to work on my yard art. That whole plan changed and grew into something much bigger once my new love, Jay, got involved. The barn, as we call it, would eventually become a new endeavor for our future. Like Jay informed me, this is not our land, this is God's land; you just bought the rights to pay the taxes. Nevertheless, we must be good stewards of his gracious property.

The hike from my condo to the barn was nineteen miles, and it included taking the ferry and a few miles of railroad. I accomplished it without a problem. On another long weekend, I took four days and hiked Garner State Park, Lost Maples, and Pedernales Falls, and then went with my sister Thelma on some trails that were fairly close to her home near Mansfield Dam. I went as far as Colorado and completed the Ouray Perimeter Trail so I could assess my abilities in the elevation difference. Remember, I live at sea level. Although it was the shortest hike I practiced, I believe it was only 5.6 miles, it was by far the most difficult and yet the most beautiful. I absolutely love Ouray and hope someday to own a tiny piece of God's paradise in those bewildering mountains.

My focus required numerous hours of overtime—nothing new to my life, but I was determined to be financially ready, and all I could do was count on myself. I saved up for the most expensive flight I've ever purchased. That in itself took hours upon hours of research and numerous email notifications from search sites that advertised "New deeply discounted pricing has just been posted by so-and-so airlines!" I researched backpacks like it was a wedding ring. Gotta find the perfect one! And the boots? That was the wedding dress! Had to fit perfectly and have just a bit of style, with ruggedness thrown into the mix. Each article of clothing was scrutinized, and each necessary item listed with its pros and cons. Even my hairbrush was a special purchase. It folded up so that it took minimal space.

When I traveled up to Colorado, I stayed with two of my dearest friends in the entire world, Henry and Andrea. I had lived with them for about six months back in the early eighties. They took me in when I was twenty-one, on the road like a free bird, and had nowhere to go. I worked two full-time jobs during those six months to save up and figure out where I was going next. Isn't that the spirit of a free bird? When I explained to Henry and Andrea what my purpose for hiking in Ouray was, they were against it. In Henry's eyes, it was far too dangerous for a female to go halfway around the world and hike by herself. They both tried to convince me not to go, and Henry even stated that if I would wait until he could arrange to take time off of work, he would go with me. I laughed. What would it take for me to convince them that their perceptions were completely misguided? It was quite easy actually. I asked them to watch a movie I had purchased that had inspired me, called *The Way*. It starred Martin Sheen and would give Henry and Andrea a better perspective of what I wanted to experience. I had made my three girls watch the movie as well, as they too were unsupportive of my adventurous endeavor. Afterward, everyone was on my side. "Okay, it looks safe. We'll let her go."

After we watched the movie, Henry handed me a gift. He placed in my hand a tiny package about one inch by three inches long. It was a rain poncho for "just in case." A small gift that would travel around the globe. A small gift that came to the rescue more than once. A small gift that offered much protection, that touched and ignited a friendship. A small gift that ended up somewhere in Warsaw, Poland. But how was that to be? Details to follow.

CHAPTER 11

Blessed

But indeed for this purpose I have raised you up, that
I may show My power in you, and that My name may
declared in all the earth.

—Exodus 9:16

During my research, I discovered I was going to need a pilgrim's
passport in order to obtain my Compostela. It shows evidence of
your pilgrimage. In every hostel or *albergue* you stay at, you acquire
a stamp as evidence you made it that far. You can also acquire stamps
at many of the bars and churches you visit along the way. It is a
storybook within itself, and every pilgrim has one. Every pilgrim has
their own special story. And every story has something important
to share.

We all have a purpose, but it is finding that purpose that we spend
our entire lives trying to figure out. I believe in my adventurous-
turned-spiritual journey I found that purpose, unbeknownst to
me at the time. It is for this reason I write, in hopes of sharing
and fulfilling that purpose. I wrote every single day during my
adventure, never realizing that those words were going to mean

something—that those repetitive words, "Oh my dear God, help me," would mean more than what they say.

The Lord has blessed me in so many ways. Countless ways. My children, my career, my friends, my few creative abilities—it's never-ending. One of those greatest blessings is my love, Jay. And to top it off, he is actually a captain. Who would have known that first the water was calling me, and then magically, this mysterious captain was thrown into the picture to help me navigate life's confusing yet joyous waters. A captain with wings upon his back. *Thank you, God. Immensely I thank you.*

When I first moved to the island, I found a boat to go fishing on so that I could learn the technique and hopefully someday master the skill. It was affordable, and they provided all the equipment. The crew was so sweet and made me feel welcomed. They taught me how to apply the bait, prevent bird's nests, when to hook 'em, and so on. I made friends rather quickly, and one of those friends was the full-time captain of the boat, Captain Bill. He was just a few years older than I was, and you could tell the boat and fishing these waters were his life and passion. Once he found out that I moved down there to learn everything I could about fishing, he took me under his wing and became my personal instructor. His experience has earned him a PhD in fishing. For the next couple of months, several years actually, I went fishing on this chartered boat and continue my fishing lessons—every chance I got. Sometime in April 2012, there was a relief captain on the boat. The deckhand introduced me to him, Captain Jay. The first time I saw him, I thought, *Well, he's kinda cute*, and I truly admired his silver hair. A lot of people on the island have silver hair. He was very kind and sweet, but that was about the extent of it. He was just another crew member.

I ran into Captain Jay occasionally at different bars and restaurants, and we shared a conversation here and there. Over the next eight months, I got to know him better and started feeling more and more comfortable with him as a friend, but nothing more than that. I loved hanging out with him, and I loved our honest conversations. In December of that year, for our hospital's Christmas party, I decided I did not want to go alone, so I asked my husband, who was overseas at the time, if I could ask my friend Jay to accompany me. He gave his approval, and I asked my friend. He accepted, and we attended. My plan was to introduce him to some of my nurse friends in order to hook them up. I thought for sure one of my friends would fall for this really sweet guy. Many of them did, but for some reason, Jay had no interest and only collected numbers. For several months thereafter, I was still trying to hook him up. Never did it cross my mind that he would have any interest in me other than as a good friend. I was far too old for him, almost nine years his senior! We continued our friendship while I was going through my divorce. We ran into each other numerous times at one of our favorite hangouts on the island, Kody's. Our friendship kept growing through our conversations and quite interesting discussions. Some of those pertained to my marriage, and I found it so peculiar that anytime I said something negative about my soon-to-be ex-husband, Jay would defend him.

I would talk about my poor husband in a negative manner, and wise-guy Jay would defend him with statements like, "Well, did you ever think about so and so?"

At one point, I asked him, "Whose side are you on?"

His response was, "I'm just giving you the male perspective."

Somehow this guy made me see things differently. He actually talked to me. He actually made sense.

I wished I could have talked to my ex like that. We should have been friends first. That's what I think we missed in the development of our relationship. I tried so many times to analyze our marriage, and for the life of me, I never figured out why we never became best friends. I think back now and understand that friendship is a huge part of a lasting and permanent relationship. It is well beyond an intimate relationship. Perhaps some people who fall in love at first sight develop the friendship part afterward. That might work as well, but I missed it all around. That is very sad.

During those months of a very simple divorce, because he was never around, I found myself thinking more and more about my friend, to the point I couldn't stop thinking about him. It was perplexing. *I have no interest in this man. Why won't he leave my head alone?* The more time I spent with him, the more I found him interesting, entertaining, amusing, hilarious at times, and he was even becoming more attractive than when I first met him. Why in the world would I think he would have any interest in me though? I would invite him over to my condo after he got off work, and we would just talk and visit. It was these conversations and his honesty that started to capture my heart. I started falling for this guy. This guy I was trying so hard to hook up with one of my friends suddenly became someone of interest to my heart. I wanted to get to know him so much deeper, yet I didn't want him to know the depths of me. I was so afraid of that. I was so afraid of letting him in to know the real and maybe not so fascinating me.

Sea Joy

A fantasy fulfilled is a fantasy no more,
So stop the tick of time and leave it at the door.
These pages are all blood-stained, please don't read this book.
I do not want to share it, don't take a second look.
Omens to the left of me, secrets to the right.
It is these simple thoughts that possess my sleepless nights.
Every wakeful moment, every single turn,
This fantasy just teases my endless, aching yearn.
It probes and pokes and tickles, yet at times it's very tense,
Leaves me so bewildered and hanging on a fence.
Don't know how to combat it, this war I cannot win,
The shadows overtake me and lost I am again.
Your words they so confuse me, I don't know what to feel.
So please just stay my fantasy and let me think you're real.

It was about two weeks before the paperwork was finalized for my divorce that I ran into Jay at the frequently visited restaurant. After our usual two drinks and conversation, we walked out to the parking lot, and for the first time, I took my chances and made a move. I leaned up to kiss him on the lips, and he turned his cheek. I was stunned, shocked, embarrassed, and humiliated at such rejection. I was crushed, thinking he really didn't have any interest in more than friendship—and who could blame him?

He responded, "You need to get your divorce, and I'm scarred."

I didn't know how to react. I just apologized, said good night, and left. I called him later that night and apologized again in hopes that it wouldn't ruin our friendship, and he replied that it wasn't necessary. Regardless, I felt so bad.

I pondered on his statement, "You need to get divorced first."

Didn't he realize that in March when I told my husband I had filed and he walked out on me instead of fighting for our marriage, at that very moment I was divorced? Why couldn't he understand that? What did he mean he was scarred? I spent many nights trying to figure this one out.

We continued our relationship, and it did not take long for us to finally get together on dates. Real dates like *she really likes him, he really likes her* kind of dates. My divorce was an easy one, but breaking down Jay's scarred wall took a great while. When I began to understand his guard, we took it at his pace, not mine. My ex-husband left me with scars as well, but I heal fast. Most men just take longer.

Jay and I got more serious in our relationship, and by October 2013, just as we were starting to establish ourselves as an item, he took a job in Galveston and moved away in November. Now I had to travel if I wanted to see and spend time with this newfound love. It was worth it—worth it to find out if this was what my heart was truly seeking. Indeed it was. He showed me respect and appreciation, which should always be a huge part of any relationship. What I found most intriguing was the fact that he actually let me in, opened up to me, and allowed me to be fully honest with my deepest thoughts. Everyone has skeletons in their closet, and when you find someone you can trust and let those skeletons out, life and relationships are so much more meaningful. It's about your vulnerability and taking a risk by opening up your mind, your heart, and your soul and letting someone in. That is love. That is true intimate love. That is the love I was beginning to experience. I asked God to help me understand and reciprocate it.

Jay had become my strongest ally in this challenging endeavor. He was there for me every step of the way. He supported all of my hikes, assuring me I was okay and safe. He took a drive down the beach on that first hike just to check on me, take pictures without my knowledge, and then send them to me! He would call me occasionally to check how far I'd made it. We'd talk every single night, not only on my practice hikes but practically every night during my journey, if I had signal. He was there for me mentally, psychologically, emotionally, and spiritually. He was my rock on the other end of the phone. God has truly blessed me excessively.

I had purchased all my equipment and bought a book, *Camino de Santiago, The Northern Route* by Laura Perazzoli and Dave Whitson. This would be my guidebook. I would count on it to help me not get lost. It was another godsend. I studied it for weeks and prepared my itinerary.

I had decided to start my travels in Bilbao. This starting point would allow me to hike approximately 420 miles. I really wanted to start at the border of Spain and France, but I was only given four weeks to hike, as I had utilized my fifth week off from work to travel to and from and a few days to get over jet lag before I had to return to work. Had I been granted six weeks off, I most certainly would have started in Irun on the border of France. It was perhaps a hidden blessing as I look back now. I planned every day in detail. From this point to that point. Exactly this many miles in exactly this amount of time. People with obsessive-compulsive behavior live by this oath: exactly and perfect. I only possess a therapeutic level of

OCD. Developing my itinerary was getting me even more excited. I submitted for my Compostela, my passport for the Camino. When it arrived, I was ecstatic. As the day for my departure approached, my excitement intensified.

I had made a master plan. I thought to myself, *Am I missing anything?*

PART II

The Journey

CHAPTER 12

And the Journey Begins

Blessed is the man whose strength is in you. Whose heart
is set on pilgrimage.

—Psalm 84:5

August 19, 2015, had finally arrived. I was ready mentally and
physically, but I had no idea that I wasn't prepared spiritually. That
thought never even crossed my mind. I thought I had always been a
strong believer in God, as I was brought up in a strong, strict Catholic
setting. I thought I knew God, but this adventure would teach me
otherwise. I can't explain the phenomenal impact this experience
had on my life. Therefore, I have to share it by taking you with me.

It began at the airport.

Jay drove me to the airport at six thirty in the morning. We
kissed goodbye and hugged like it was the last one. I could tell he
was proud of me in his eyes and his words.

"Call me every chance you get. Please be safe. I love you."

I love this man immensely. I was going to make him proud
of this old lady. He drove away as I reorganized my backpack and
noticed I had left the top zipper unzipped. Apparently, a few items
had fallen out in the truck, so I immediately called him and asked

him to turn around. A few minutes later, he was at my side again. Not only did I retrieve my items, but I got another hug and one more lengthy goodbye kiss. That was so worth the time.

As I was sitting in the terminal waiting for my flight, I began to pray. I began to pray because it was just hitting me that I was traveling to a foreign country on the other side of the world, alone, with all the supplies I needed to survive for a month on my back. What was I thinking and getting myself into? Now I started understanding why so many of my friends and family had questioned my judgment. For a moment, I felt alone, and then I realized I was not alone. His presence in my mind, heart, and soul overtook that all-alone feeling. God and I had a heart-to-heart conversation internally. I also talked to my beloved father in the spiritual form. I asked them both to accompany me on this trip. I was just a little afraid—not much but a little. I needed my own prayer, so I took pen to paper and wrote it down so I wouldn't forget it.

My Journey's Prayer

Grace me with your presence Lord,
with every step I take.
I give my every breath to you
on this journey I must make.
Please take my hand and lead the way
and please help me to see
That every day I wake and sleep
You'll be next to me.
I will pray as I walk
in these foreign lands
For all the ones I dearly love,
I leave them in your hands.
For I have faith and love and hope
in prayers I have shown,
And knowing you'll be next to me,

I shall never be alone.

As I read what I had written, I felt so much better. I smiled and decided I needed to share it. I got on Facebook and posted this prayer for all my friends and family, to reassure them I would not be walking alone on this exciting trip. It was mostly for my own reassurance that I would never be alone and therefore had nothing to fear. I wanted my family to know I was going to be all right.

Dallas airport never fails me. It always participates in Murphy's Law when I have a connecting flight there. Sure enough, something happened, and my flight was cancelled. I had to find a different route. I was at my wit's end because the attendant at the desk was not helpful at all. I figured it out on my own and found a flight, but it would take me to Florida, which would extend my already lengthy itinerary. I believe everything happens for a reason.

I was fortunate enough to sit next to a lovely lady named Mary, from Miami. We struck up a conversation, and when I informed her where I was headed, she was so intrigued with my upcoming pilgrimage. She was into health foods and fitness as her livelihood, so she gave me several protein bars and energy drink mixes to carry on my journey. That was so kind of her. Just as we were descending into Miami, she did something even more special.

She grabbed my hand and said, "Let's say a prayer for your journey."

I was caught off guard and was immediately overwhelmed with joy. "Of course! I would love that!"

"It would bring me great pleasure," she said as she begin her prayer with the Lord's blessing.

I was overwhelmed with joy because here we were, two complete strangers, making a spiritual connection thousands of feet up in the air and saying a prayer. Wow. That was so awesome. She was so kind and thoughtful to pray for my safety and success.

Above the white clouds,

Mary my angel sent he.
God sent her to me.

On August 20th, I landed in Madrid, Spain. I had a long layover and was killing time, charging my phone and reviewing my guidebook. There was a young man sitting close by, and I introduced myself, as he had a backpack and was charging his phone as well. Sure enough, he had just completed his Camino journey and was heading home back to Italy. His name was David, and he shared with me several suggestions and recommendations to consider throughout my hike—stuff like Wi-Fi connections, bag weight, foot care, meals, and so on. I did my best to absorb it all. He was so helpful, and I greatly appreciated his time.

By the metal wings
David to share many things
Experience he brings.

From Madrid, I flew to Santiago. This was where my journey would conclude, so I had scheduled a round-trip ticket to and from Santiago to the States. I purchased a one-way ticket from Santiago to Bilbao, where I would start. I had made reservations at a hotel, which I was able to find, but unfortunately, when I went to check in, they informed me I hadn't called twenty-four hours prior to my arrival to secure my spot. What? I had no idea that was the routine for the hotels there. It was for the albergues. She explained to me that they only have twenty-two beds, and they release them if they're not secured. I always learn the hard way. Well, at least she gave me some ideas about where I might be able to find a bed, but it would not be anywhere close to the center of the city where the cathedral was, as all rooms stayed booked close to 100 percent of the time. *Great, just great.* She suggested a hostel about thirty minutes away, but I would have to learn how to ride the bus. Thank goodness I can speak Spanish, not proper Spanish but more like Tex-Mex. I can get across what I need to say, but I have to ask some people to slow down if they are talking too fast, as it takes my brain a little more time than the average Hispanic from Texas to comprehend appropriately. She gave me instructions on how to find the bus, which number to look for, and where to get off. She truly was helpful.

I managed to find the hostel and was pleasantly surprised that it only cost six euros. That was a savings of sixteen euros! Go me! I paid my debt and found my first bunk. I unpacked and decided to go exploring, as I had plenty of time to kill. I found a cute little restaurant and ordered what they call *Menu del Dia*, which means meal of the day. Come to find out practically all restaurants have the Menu del Dia for a very reasonable price. This particular one was ten euros (approximately $8.50). This meal deal included an appetizer, a bottle of wine even if you're dining alone, or you could choose beer but were limited to one or two, a main dish with several sides, and a dessert. Most cost between eight to twelve euros, and were always well worth it. I explored the mall across the street and walked around several blocks just checking things out.

I found my way back to the albergue and prepared for a shower. When I discovered it was a community shower, I was stunned. This situation had never even crossed my mind. Although I was uncomfortable and somewhat embarrassed, I pretended not to be. I hadn't taken a shower with a bunch of women since high school, which seemed like a century ago. I got over it soon enough, finished my routine, and crawled into bed. I decided to Facebook my friends and family and share my pictures and what I had experienced thus far. I decided that I would do that every night, share my journey, mostly for my sister, Thelma. I was the adventurous one of the two, and she very rarely gets to travel due to her job, so I wanted to bring her with me. What better way than Facebook? I was so excited about flying to Bilbao in the morning that it was difficult to fall asleep. That plus the fact that I was sleeping in a room with about ten other people, most of whom were snoring. It was like a symphony, with an orchestra and a conductor snoring in unison, all in tune with the other. I smiled and finally drifted off to sleep.

The following morning, August 21st, I got up early, packed my backpack, and headed to the bus stop to find my way to the airport. I got there in plenty of time and had no hiccups getting myself to Bilbao. Once I arrived in Bilbao, I rode the bus from the airport to midtown. Wouldn't you know it: on the very first day of my arrival, I walked in the wrong direction. This would be the first of many. After walking about ten maybe fifteen blocks in the wrong direction, I finally started asking for directions, showing friendly people on the street the address of the hostel I was looking for. After several attempts, one kind person concluded that indeed I was walking the opposite way, so I turned around and walked back where I had started. I eventually found the correct street, and there I went again turning right when I was supposed to turn left. Maybe this was just practice for what I was going to be up against. Finally I figured it out and turned back around the other way. I finally found my hostel! What should have been a fifteen-minute walk ended up being more like an hour and a half. Just my luck. It was okay though because I did find my way, with a few smiles and laughing at myself en route.

I was placed in an all-girl dorm room with three sets of bunk beds. Four very young girls, in their early twenties maybe, were stationed in the room. They were obviously vacationing and there in Bilbao to have a really good time. I introduced myself, as did each of them while they were primping for a night on the town. One of the girls named Pat, who was stunningly beautiful, stated she was from Barcelona. I had been to Barcelona once before and had fallen in love with that beautiful city, so we had a short and pleasant conversation. The other three teeny boppers were from Madrid. They kind of reminded me of myself thirty some odd years ago.

> Oh how fair is she,
> Pat the adventurous one,
> Naïve and so young!

The girls had left for the night, and I studied my guidebook with anticipation. It was about ten, maybe ten thirty when the last bed was filled by a young Chinese lad named Charlie from Washington, DC. The staff placed Charlie in our dorm because it was the last bed in the hostel. He certainly didn't mind sleeping with a bunch of girls, as he too was in his early twenties. I could immediately tell something was wrong though, as Charlie appeared to be very confused and frustrated. I introduced myself and asked him what was wrong. He stated he had started walking the Camino this morning but had gotten lost and ended up about five miles off the trail. He had been walking with a friend of his. It had started raining and had gotten dark, and the night had become dreadfully dreary. His friend decided to pitch his tent and spend the night out in the rain, but Charlie didn't want any part of that, so he managed to find his way back to Bilbao to start over. It was an entirely wasted day, which unfortunately was his first, perhaps his last the way he was sounding. He told me his father had recommended this walk and encouraged him to experience it. I, for some reason, interpreted it like the parent was sending his child off to a boarding school, and the child didn't want to go but had to. I felt so sorry for him. I informed him that I was just going to get started in the morning, as it would be my first official day of walking. I told him I had purchased a guidebook and showed it to him, letting him know that I was counting on it to help me not get so lost. I showed him the specifics and how this book informed me not only how far to go but what signs to look for, where the nearest bar or albergue was, how many beds were there, and so on. Charlie started looking at my book, and suddenly his demeanor changed. It looked like a tiny bit of hope was entering his mind.

"Oh wow. I wish I had known these books were available. I would have bought one. Do you mind if I write a few notes to help me get started?"

Of course I did not mind. It made my heart happy that I could help someone in need, but more importantly, my heart smiled when his frustration turned to hope. He turned page after page, studying and reading. When he finished, he handed me back my book and couldn't thank me enough. Little did I know this little book was like a little Bible of hope.

> A tear in his eye,
> Charlie's so lost but will try
> And still say goodbye.

Again I had trouble falling asleep from all the excitement. I vaguely remember the girls coming back in well after two o'clock in the morning. I do recall though how funny I thought it was that they were stripping off their clothes to get into their nighties, not realizing that there was a gentleman in the last bunk. I giggled inside. I think he was a bit embarrassed and just hid under his blankets. Yeah, right.

CHAPTER 13

Day 1: August 22nd, Bilbao to Pobeña - 16.2 Miles

> Trust in the Lord with all your heart And lean not on your own understanding; In all your ways acknowledge Him, And He shall direct your paths.
>
> —Proverbs 3:5-6

Needless to say, I eagerly got up early, around six, quietly packed the few things I had utilized to prepare for the day, and slipped out of the room in hopes of not waking any of my roommates. Today was the first official day of my pilgrimage, my hike, my journey, my adventure. I just couldn't believe it. I was overexcited. The numerous sculptured lampposts brightly lit up the quiet city streets. I admired Bilbao's buildings and architecture, almost like an outdoor museum. The slowly lifting fog was waltzing with the streetlights' perplexing glow. I couldn't get enough of this gorgeous setting, so peaceful and quiet. The parties were over, and the housekeepers of the city were ending their shifts as the garbage trucks' music lingered in the background.

Today's chore was learning how to find all the different way-marks, shells, arrows, and signs. I decided that every time I saw one, I would thank the good Lord, kiss my diamond cross that I would wear every single day, and feel reassured I was on the right path. Sometimes it got confusing in the bigger cities, but it wouldn't take long. If I felt unsure, I would stop a stranger, ask which direction, and they would gladly point me the right way. Even in this dissipating darkness, I was feeling comfortable and confident.

I followed a lengthy curved bridge over a sparkling star-lit river. I found my first arrow across the street from an albergue that I wish I had known about. It was still silent as I passed by. Maybe I started too early. I questioned myself. As I would later learn, yes, six o'clock is far too early for pilgrims. Most start stirring at about seven. Albergues and hostels request your departure between eight and nine at the latest. I crossed the street from the sleeping albergue onto a walkway next to the river known as the Rio Nervion de Bilbao. I had chosen this route that followed the river for several miles instead of through the middle of town. I watched the sunrise and the minimal traffic on the waterway and listened to the noise that started to increase as the sun kissed the horizon and it turned the light switch to the "on" position. Daybreak was here.

I was carrying between twenty-one and twenty-two pounds on my back. My water bladder was full to capacity, and I had treats waiting for any unexpected or needed breaks. This was so super cool. I admired everything around me, even the graffiti on the buildings and fences, like they were canvases of some artistic lost souls. I passed a boat that appeared shipwrecked and abandoned, which made me think about my sweet captain at home. It crossed my mind, *Oh what he could do with that boat!* I made it to Las Arenas in no time. After a few more miles, I approached the Vizcaya Bridge cable ferry, aka Puente Colgante, which translates to Hanging Bridge. It was built in 1893 and was a ferry that transported vehicles and pedestrians across the river above the water via hanging cable cars. Extraordinary! I had to figure out the mechanics of the ticketing system. I can't read Spanish, so I was utterly lost, but I could figure out where coins went and tried a few. After several attempts, it worked, and I got my ticket! What luck! Thank you, Lord. *I probably overpaid for all I know!*

It was an awesome ride. Upon arrival on the other side, I took a left, and a few blocks later, I arrived at a busy public square, the city's central plaza. A few vendors were selling beautiful flowers, and hanging baskets full of flowers showered the square. I had lots of trouble trying to locate the next arrow and follow directions via my guidebook, and for some reason, maybe my poor navigational skills, I was just getting more confused. I went ahead and chose a route, and it didn't take long to figure out it was the wrong way. I stopped a nice-looking gentleman and asked him for directions. He simply pointed to the opposite side of the square, which was now half a block away, and told me to take a left. I thanked him kindly and continued on my merry way. I took the left and encountered something quite peculiar, a moving walkway that took you up the hill. Pretty cool, especially because it was uphill. I enjoyed the lift. I found my way quite easily the rest of the day. As I started to exit this quaint little town, I was walking in probably one of the last residential areas, and an elderly gentleman who was taking a stroll with a buddy stopped me and asked me where I was from. I said, "Texas," instead of saying the United States. It just came out automatically and that was how I would respond the rest of my Camino. It's so funny how every single person who asked me knew immediately where the state of Texas was located. His eyes widened, and his smile broadened when I answered him.

This sweet little old man made friendly conversation in Spanish, and before my departure, he said, "Aqui, un flor para una peregrina bonita," (Here, a flower for a beautiful pilgrim), and presented me with a flower for my hair! "Buen Camino!" (Good way).

I smiled, thanked him, and continued my wonderful journey. I placed that beautiful flower in my hair just as my grandma Saldaña would have done. It was so nice to hear "Buen Camino!" from strangers all day long.

There were a few times I didn't feel as confident as I should have and would simply ask God to show me a sign. Sure enough, it never took long. He accompanied me every step of the way, just as I had prayed.

Arrival to Pobeña would conclude with 37,953 steps, 16.2 miles, and 1,158 calories burned according to my Fit App. These numbers were fun to keep up with, but eventually, they would become meaningless. I was the first one to arrive at the albergue, and it was not even open yet. Come to find out, 3:00 p.m. was a standard opening time for most albergues, so I had a little time to kill. I waited for a short while, and a few more pilgrims showed up, also proud of their timing. We left our backpacks alongside the building next to the door in a first-come, first-served line and went to explore the little town. I found a cute little restaurant and had a beer and a *pincho* (a snack). Some parts of the country call them tapas. This eventually became my favorite pastime, treating myself to a beer and pincho upon arrival to the next destination.

By the time I returned to the albergue, the backpack line had quadrupled. The doors were opened by the *hospitalero*, the term used for the keepers of the albergues, who were usually volunteers. We all checked in and claimed our bunks. Dinner was served at seven, and there was much socializing and sharing experiences of the Camino. Endless smiles flooded the extended table, as did contagious laughter and foreign chitchat. This was so lovely. So many strangers at a table sharing a meal and a harmonious moment together. If only the world could exist in such manner.

I couldn't wait to share day 1 with my sister on Facebook. I had taken so many pictures not only on my phone but also on Jay's GoPro camera. I simply could not take enough pictures of this stunning, beautiful country. I called and said good night to the love of my life, and again, I fell asleep with a smile.

CHAPTER 14

Day 2: August 23rd, Pobeña to Castro-Urdiales - 12.3 Miles

He has made everything beautiful in its time. Also He has put eternity in their hearts, except that no one can find out the work that God does from beginning to end.

—Ecclesiastes 3:11

Today would be a short day. I only walked 4.5 hours. The entire time, with each step I found myself falling more and more in love with Spain. The serene scenes were never-ending. The mountains and rock cliffs lined up against the beaches were stunningly beautiful. The walkways and paths were so incredibly bewitching and charming. I was fascinated by the beauty they each possessed. The boardwalks were finely decorated, and the plazas were saturated with clinging vines and colorful flowers. Spain was melting my heart. I stopped so many times just to take pictures and absorb the splendid surroundings and gorgeous views. The beaches, the reason I had chosen this route, were elegant and enticing. The waves were not angry but rather kind. The water's color was the deep hue of blue you would expect on a postcard. I wanted to put a swimsuit on and go jump in those radiant waters. Unfortunately, a swimsuit was not on the list of essential items. *Why?* I thought. I realized I had not planned for the time to stop and enjoy the water. I remember at one point fishing crossed my mind, but that takes a least half a day if you really want to enjoy it.

There was this man-made tunnel I had to walk through going through the side of a mountain toward Onton, and while I was walking through it, I thought to myself how unsafe it was, kind of like exploring an ice cave under a glacier—just a bit unsafe. They were using wooden beams to hold it up or give it strength. How in the world could anyone rely on wood to prevent a tunnel from collapsing? I accelerated my pace. Upon exiting, my breath was taken away! Wow, the view was stunning. This scene was precisely the reason I chose the Northern Route, to experience this mesmerizing picture. I got the privilege of walking on this city's promenade boardwalk on the beach and wished for a moment that I could live there. I received so many "Buen Caminos" in this section of town it was incredible. These people were so friendly. Even the dogs being taken on their walks behaved like it was the socially correct thing to do.

When I arrived in Castro-Urdiales, I located the albergue fairly easily, and again I was the first one to arrive. This one was located behind an old Toro stadium, which was no longer utilized for that function. Nevertheless, it was still a beautiful structure. The city was colorful, and it was enjoyable just strolling through it. A young pilgrim arrived shortly after I did, and he introduced himself as Nacho. He was from Madrid and extremely friendly. Several others arrived, one by one, two by two. Before long, we were scattered throughout the yard. He was straightforward when they opened the albergue and informed everyone that I was the first one in line. I didn't realize that albergues have a format for allowing pilgrims to occupy their beds. You must be in line when they open, which again is usually around three o'clock. They take walkers first, whoever gets there first, followed by cyclists. Once they run out of beds, you have to figure out where you're going to stay if you didn't get one. Realizing that this was the unwritten rule, it had a slight impact on my desire to reach my destination even sooner. Good thing I didn't bring a fishing pole.

After we were all checked in, as pilgrims continued to arrive, Nacho asked me if I wanted to go have a beer and a bite to eat. I gladly accepted, and we were off to find a place. Nacho, in his mid-twenties, worked at IBM. He only took off work one week at a time to do the Camino, and this was his second leg. It would eventually take him five years, and he was barely on year number two. I learned a lot more about Spain and also about Nacho. We had a wonderful conversation about work, life, and what we enjoy doing on our time off. Adventures was on both of our lists. Of course it crossed my mind how nice it would be if I could have introduced him to one of my daughters. He would have been such a dream catch. I liked my new friend. He made me laugh so much. He was also intrigued by my background from Texas and had many questions, which I gladly answered. I should have worn my cowboy hat to Spain; that would have been entertaining. I don't recall ever seeing a cowboy hat on my hike. The other thing that stood out was I never saw any trucks on the roads or in the towns I walked through. Oh my, what a different world it is in Texas. You can't go a mile down the road without seeing at least ten or more. We walked back to the albergue. I made my phone calls, played on my phone, studied my guidebook, Facebooked, and eventually drifted off into a happy dream.

Castro-Urdiales

CHAPTER 15

Day 3: August 24th, Castro-Urdiales to Laredo - 16.26 Miles

If you abide in Me, and My words abide in you, you will ask what you desire, and it shall be done for you.

—John 15:7

I'm beginning to make it a habit to be the first one up in the mornings. Even so, I try to be very quiet. I believe it's because I still fear not getting a bed by the end of the day, and I don't want to encounter that situation. I'm on a nice little high establishing my routine, which makes any OCDer happy. My water bladder is full, my camera is ready, and my spirit is ready to sore across this fabulous nation another day. The gorgeous, long, and winding roads are calm and serene. The pastures are inviting, and the herds of cattle and horses are mellow on this dazzling morning. The churches are popping up frequently today, and I say a silent prayer as I pass each one. How blessed and fortunate am I to experience this country that God has truly kissed.

The coast lines on today's Camino were overwhelming with

beauty. They were beyond words, just so magical. I was beginning to learn that when you visit a country on vacation, you truly can't appreciate it the same way unless you walk it. Get intimate with its dirt roads, its pastures, its people out in the countryside. I passed a beautiful horse grazing on the side of a hill with the sea painted behind it. I paused and admired it. He lifted his head while still chomping on the green grass and perhaps admired me in return. If he could have spoken, I'm sure he would have asked me where I was from. I smiled, took a picture, and he continued his happiness. I counted my blessings to be afforded such beauty. After several breathtaking miles, I encountered Nacho and another pilgrim at about ten in the morning along the Camino. We pulled over at a cute little bar, Bar El Pontarron. I enjoyed an ice-cold Coke and a snack with my two new friends outside on the patio. I didn't want to extend my visit, as I knew how slowly I was going, being so camera happy. Shortly after I departed, Nacho yelled to me. I turned around, and he pointed me in the other direction. Naturally. Thank you Nacho. I continued my walk as I cheerfully passed the reassuring arrows and signs, kissing my cross along the way. Uncontrollable smiles and sheer happiness with every step. I felt like skipping, but that doesn't look so cool at fifty-five, plus, I had twenty-plus pounds on my back weighing me down. Postcard scenes were abundant today. Spain's immaculate countryside is simply a dream.

I had previously made arrangements that every so many days I would stay in a hotel instead of an albergue or hostel and appreciate their services, especially getting a good night's sleep. Today would be my first encounter, and my only concern was how far off the Camino it would be. How would I find it? I was getting more and more concerned as I was approaching the city of Laredo. So I prayed. And with every few steps, I prayed some more—and more, knowing my nature concerning directions. *Please, Lord, help me find this place. My feet are starting to ache just a bit.* Just as I was heading down a steep hill, I captured a glimpse of the city of Laredo. She was stunning. Such a gorgeous sight from that steep hill. So I stopped to take a picture, several actually. Just as I turned to put my camera away, I looked up the left side of the hill, and there she was! I couldn't believe it! My hotel was right there, staring at me in the face! Had I not stopped to take that picture, I would have totally missed it. Who knows how many miles I would have had to walk and turn back around to find it. My concern melted away, and my relief and smiles took over. I was comforted knowing he had answered my prayers so quickly. I was so amazed at this coincidence I couldn't stop smiling all the way to the entrance.

While purchasing my room, the sweet lady informed me of the restaurant hours. I absorbed the personality of the bar and restaurant: the hanging cow legs dripping their grease into the little cups, the decorations, the smells, the bottles lined against the mirrored wall behind the bar. Just my kind of place. I loved it. I unpacked my bags and enjoyed a private shower. My balcony, even though tiny, allowed me to overlook the city of Laredo and the neighboring bodies of water.

City of Laredo

Just stunning. I couldn't get enough. Dinner, needless to say, was awesome. The atmosphere was so … Spain. Friendly, inviting, and comfortable. Back in my room, I relaxed on the balcony, enjoying a beer. I Facebooked before I slipped into a peaceful sleep, without the snoring, sneezing, coughing, and flatus. Yes, peace.

CHAPTER 16

Day 4: August 25th, Laredo to Guemes - 21.7 Miles

Be anxious for nothing, but in everything by prayer and supplication, with thanksgiving, let your requests be made known to God.

—Philippians 4:6

Sunrise was greeted by my alarm clock. I felt I had perfected my wake time. I jumped out of bed, eager to get back on the Camino. I found my way to this incredible city by the water as my hotel was on the border of the entrance to Laredo. The boardwalk was just beholding and picturesque as the glittering sunlight tiptoed across the mirrored waters of Playa de Laredo o de Salvé. I had called my mom the night before to give her an update of my adventure, and she informed me that my little brother, Aaron, was having lots of issues with his back, to the point he could not walk any longer. He was in dire need of surgery, and it was scheduled for today. Therefore, I promised her that I would dedicate a special step for him as soon as

I stepped on the beach, and I did. I had to stop and take a picture of my hiking boot embedded in the sand and dedicate it to him with prayers for a speedy recovery. I posted it on Facebook, requesting prayers. Today I would walk for him. I prayed to God that he would watch over him and help him get well soon.

The promenade in Laredo along the beach was surreal. More and more, I loved this country. I knew I was going to have to cross the peninsula of Bahia de Santoña via ferry to get to my next destination, but I over-prepared, not surprising, and got to the ticket office an hour before they opened. No worries. Many pilgrims arrived right behind me. As more hikers gathered, with natural pilgrim behavior, we started forming a line waiting for the boat's arrival. My walk today, for some bizarre reason, was really starting to affect my feet in a negative manner. They were really starting to hurt me midday. Perhaps I was pushing myself too hard, as today was a 21.7-mile day. I walked until about 5:00 p.m., and my feet were really feeling it by the time I arrived at my next destination, Guemes. Regardless, my mind and body were so alive, eager, energetic, and excited by all the surrounding beauty, the abundant sights, and the friendly sounds of Spain. The scents and smells of old Spain took all the attention away from the aching that was slowly encroaching on these size sevens.

I ran into Nacho again and a few other familiar faces as we waited for the ferry. The ride to Santoña was so enjoyable—the sun glistening on the water, the peaceful encapsulation of nature surrounding me. So engulfed in God's presence was I. I made a few new friends en route. An absolutely beautiful German girl name Neoneé introduced herself. She was probably late twenties, early thirties maybe. Throughout the day, she kept passing me by.

> Kindness in her eye,
> Neoneé would pass me by,
> Such lost butterfly.

Upon arrival at Santoña, I started slowly, somewhat because of my feet. They were starting to talk to me, but the sights and sounds deterred any thoughts of discomfort. All the other pilgrims started at their own rapid pace, and I began to lag behind a bit early. I hiked many beach miles today, which was quite challenging in hiking boots, but before I reached this fantasy beach, I had to climb a mountain-like, treacherous, rocky hill. It presented itself to me with scorching claws and an evil dare, even more so with twenty pounds on my back. I had to utilize all fours to get over certain parts, but I managed. Once I reached the other side, upon descending this jungle, it opened up to a spectacular beach ... naturally! I had built up quite a sweat and decided to unzip my pants and convert them to shorts—you know, that cool kind of hiking pants. Unfortunately, I got the zipper stuck on one side that I couldn't reach easily, and as I looked up, another pilgrim was passing me by. I quickly asked her if she would kindly help me out and get the zipper unstuck.

She smiled and gladly stated, "Of course."

Her name was Clare, and she was from Barcelona. I thanked her from the bottom of my heart, as that simple, kind gesture made me feel so much better physically and mentally. We both enjoyed a short break and a quick conversation.

Today was endless pictures. Practically every minute or two, I had to stop and take a couple. How, I wondered, do so many people in this world live in gloomy, dreadful, or lonely places when the world is so full of such beautiful and blessed options? Figure it out. Find out the place that makes you happy and go live there. Find a way to go live there. Life is too short to live elsewhere. Be wise. Just figure it out. I realized that is exactly what I had done by moving to my island.

Every step was becoming more and more painful for some bizarre reason. I couldn't understand it. I recall as I was approaching Guemes how dreamlike it was. From afar, it appeared to be a mansion upon a hill. I smiled, realizing that was to be my destination at day's end. I recall embracing the pastures and the homes surrounding this hill. The cows, the hay, and the fields engulfed all my senses.

While entering the welcoming gate, I was greeted with a friendly smile, a cookie, and a glass of water. How very sweet and kind this gesture was.

This albergue was different—very different, as I would soon find out. This one had a special story behind it. Why was it so different? Was it the beauty of its pleasant setting on the hill, the greeter, the atmosphere? What made this place so special?

Again I was blessed with a single bed. The rest were all bunks in this particular dorm. Eight other pilgrims would share my room for the night. There were several other dorms in this albergue, so I knew there were going to be many pilgrims there for the night. My bed was right next to a window that I could look out of, so I continued admiring the surrounding countryside's beauty. Thank you, Lord. I unpacked, showered, and dressed for dinner. Prior to dinner though, they held a welcoming meeting in the library. All of us pilgrims sat on a bench that encircled this great room. A gentleman introduced himself and welcomed all of us. He found someone in the group that would be willing to translate all that he was to say in English. A brave soul volunteered his services as he raised his hand. He was introduced to the group. This translator just happened to be Caesar, a gentleman who slept above me a few nights ago. The one that didn't let me sleep. The one that tossed and turned in his squeaky bunk all night. He did a very good job translating and even made it humorous. We all enjoyed the laughter.

They began telling us about the history of this albergue and of the founder, Ernesto Bustio. He wasn't present during this storytelling gathering, but we would get an opportunity to meet him later that evening at dinner or thereafter. The history of Ernesto was truly fascinating. His travels, his determination, his way of life, and his contributions to the community surrounding him were astounding. His dedication to helping pilgrims on the Camino was so admirable. Everything I heard was just so positive, so Christian-like, so Godly. I fell in love with this elderly, white-haired man who devoted his entire life to helping others. He converted his home to this albergue that accommodates at least sixty-eight pilgrims. Plus, there is overflow spare space on the floor so that no one is turned away.

After the extremely entertaining storytelling session, we met in a large communal kitchen. We had bread and butter with cream of pumpkin soup as an appetizer. I don't even like pumpkin, but I could certainly have had several bowls of that. It was delicious. The main course consisted of a tomato-based soup, which was also worth seconds, but I refrained. Along with this was the typical wine everyone drinks in Spain and some very engaging conversations from all around the world. Just my table alone had people from Madrid, Barcelona, London, Germany, and of course Texas. An extremely lovely lady, probably in her late sixties, who was from London, England, was sitting at my table. I envied her silver hair; every strand of it was in perfect position. She reminded me of the older lady who starred in the movie *The Notebook*. Her accent, as all British accents are, was so ultimately cool.

I spoke to a young lady from Madrid that I had met earlier that morning. It was Clara, that sweet little angel who helped me unzip my pants when I reached the bottom of that treacherous hill. I got the opportunity to get to know Clara just a little bit more. She was twenty-four years old. Her parents were not happy she went on the walk by herself. I told her my children shared the same view with me coming over here on the other side of the world, alone. We were one of the same with adventure.

> I just could not reach.
> Clara was sweet as a peach,
> Zipped me at the beach.

I met a couple from Madrid that was just precious. They were so in love. Such a cute couple. I would run into them again in the next town, where we would spend more time together. I also ran into Neoneé, but she was staying in a different dorm room. After a fabulous dinner, those interested in listening and learning more about the history of this albergue were invited to join and follow the teacher/host to a chapel established behind the main building. Must have been twenty maybe twenty-five of us who followed, eagerly waiting for more intriguing stories.

Upon entrance to this small prayer room, Ernesto greeted us. He reminded me of Santa Claus but much healthier. Again the speaker found another volunteer to interpret. I held back from volunteering to spare embarrassment.

The relatively small chapel consisted of six walls. Benches were built against the walls that encircled this entire space. Each wall had a painting drawn on it, and each had its own story, yet they all flowed together. Ernesto told us about the artist who came from South America. He hand-painted this story as a gift. It was an interesting and educational story, but the two walls that captured my fascination showed several pilgrims carrying another pilgrim of a darker skin tone. Whether it represented Hispanic or black didn't matter; it represented a minority. The story here was how over the years, we as a people have come together to help each other out in times of need. On the next wall was a table of pilgrims having a feast, and Ernesto continued with the flow of the story. He shared with us regarding a black pilgrim who visited many years ago, and as he was telling the story, the gentleman voiced his opinion. He brought to the visitors' and Ernesto's attention that he acknowledged being helped and accepted that help in the first painting, but in the second, he had no seat at the table. My mind wandered off like it often does into my own thought process, thinking, *Well, then make yourself a seat!* That was the first thought that popped into my head. I'm sure that pilgrim did not intend to make it sound like he was complaining but rather just bringing the issue to light. I, on the other hand, felt empowered at that moment. I felt empowered because I felt like I had made my own seat at the table. The table of life, in success of a career, a family, a purpose. If you're not going to be invited to sit at the table, then take the bull by the horns and create your own seat, buddy. I felt that, even being a minority and a female, my determination and hard work had created my own seat at the table. No more whining, okay?

The conversation was so very deep, so very meaningful and full of life secrets that only privileged pilgrims were honored to be exposed to it. I adored this man. He was an angel in the flesh. So humble and such a servant of God. After the stories ended at approximately nine o'clock, we began flowing out of the chapel. I greeted Ernesto and introduced myself. I felt that he was a disciple of the ages, spreading the love that God instilled within him. I made it back to my room, happy and satisfied with the events of the day. I felt so fulfilled even though my feet were aching something awful. I figured I just needed a good night's sleep, and they would feel much better in the morning. My nightly ritual was completed in darkness, and I fell asleep in harmony.

CHAPTER 17

Day 5: August 26th, Guemes to Santander - 12.6 Miles

Confess your trespasses to one another, and pray for one another, that you may be healed. The effective fervent prayer of a righteous man avails much.

—James 5:16

Morning came much too fast. My dorm room had one tiny bathroom, and I had to share it with eight other pilgrims; therefore, I waited my turn. I got ready as fast as I could and went back to the communal kitchen for breakfast. I loved this place—the long tables, the sincere friendliness of all the volunteers, just the total atmosphere. I visited again with my new friends before I loaded up my backpack and began my early departure. The experience at Ernesto's albergue was unbelievable, leaving such an incredible, positive impression upon me.

I had spoken to Neoneé, my friend from Germany, whom I found out later was an atheist. She found something negative about the entire evening—the storytelling, the albergue, and mostly

Ernesto. She felt that they built him and his story up just for more donations. She looked at it more like bragging about his greatness and accomplishments. I was appalled. I couldn't believe anyone would find anything negative about that wonderful place. But she managed. She focused on the donation aspect of it. This was a free albergue. There was no charge for pilgrims; they only took donations. Therefore, after breakfast, they passed around the bucket, and you gave as you desired. Most albergues charge between five and twelve euros for a bed. Some charge nothing at all. I willing gave triple because of my appreciation for the evening and the education. I had a comfortable bed, two fabulous meals, and great entertainment. I think she just passed the bucket. I prayed for her, in hope that God would shed some light in her direction. She had a powerful impact on my thoughts for the day. Although I ran into Neoneé four or five times during these early days, I thought and prayed for her often.

> He who believes in Him is not condemned; but he who does not believe is condemned already, because he has not believed in the name of the only begotten Son of God.
>
> —John 3:18

I would run into several atheists throughout my journey, but my friend Neoneé would represent them all. She and those she represented made my heart so heavy. It saddened me that there are so many people who do not know the joy of God in their lives. I simply could not digest that people deny his love. Oh, how lost they must be. She is such a beautiful and intelligent girl, which made it even more difficult to understand her lack of understanding what faith is.

The Lost Butterfly

It weighs so heavy on my heart, the part
that you cannot and will not believe.

No soul have you? So easily deceived.
I will not tread your waters but in your daze, respect my ways.
What have I to wonder if your mind refuses to ponder?
Should I push my Lord, your bread? Or allow them to be misled?
I pray a miracle to be thrown before their eyes. Leave them
mesmerized. Watch them grow, help them to know
that you walk above our comprehension.

This morning was magical. The dew on the pasture was glistening like diamonds. The horses and cows were gently painted on the golden horizon. The clouds and the sunrise were so incredible. Had time allowed, I would have stood still and watched the creation of the day. I felt good, and I was happy. I felt so lucky and so blessed. I grabbed my cross and kissed it as I had done so many times before.

I recalled last night as I lay in my bed, watching the moon from my window, that my feet hurt. They really ached, terribly. The ache continued this morning, but certainly it was tolerable. The sights and sounds of Spain—I just simply could not absorb enough of its beauty, and that took my mind off the unwelcoming ache.

The trails were so cool. Trails on top of cliffs, overlooking the gorgeous blue waters down below. It was a short walk today, only about 12.6 enjoyable miles. I had to ride another ferry. This one took me to Santander. I rode on the very back, enjoying the pristine blue water. Working my way through this town, I was certain I had visited it before with my ex-husband. I recalled having a difficult time finding a hotel, and when we did, it was at an astronomical cost. One hundred euros for a tiny room that barely fit a full-size bed. You had to walk sideways to get into the bed. I laughed at the memory.

I found the albergue without too much difficulty. There were about four or five pilgrims who had arrived before me, so of course the line was forming. Since they didn't open until three, I left my backpack with the hospitalero, just as everyone else did, and went to discover Santander. I ran into Neoneé again, and we had lunch together at one of the street cafés. I really enjoyed the sidewalk cafés. Spain is infested with them. I also enjoyed Neoneé's company. It was during this conversation I discovered her atheist beliefs. I respect the choice everyone has to believe or not, but I really wasn't sure she wasn't respecting my choice. I didn't challenge her but rather focused on the blessings he has bestowed on me and how much more joyful and fulfilling life is when he is a part of it. She remained a bit negative, like she wasn't happy with her life, which shouldn't have surprised me. We discussed work and family life, and I again reiterated how God is a big part of my world. I understand believing is a choice, but wouldn't it be wiser to believe and it not be, rather than to not believe and it be?

We concluded our lunch and headed back to the albergue, where I checked in and claimed my bunk. Unfortunately, I ended up on a top bunk this time. Can't win them all. I ran into the couple, Romeo and Juliet, I mean Oscar and Natalie, that sat at my table in Guemes. There claimed the bunk below mine. After settling in, they invited me to go explore Santander and have dinner with them. I gladly accepted the invite, and we were soon joined by another friend of theirs, Vance. All three of them were from Madrid. I believe they wanted my company because I spoke good English, and I was from Texas. I encountered that feeling many times throughout my trip, as Texas just seems to be such an interest throughout the world. I think John Wayne had a bit to do with it.

> You included me
> Oscar and Nat, naturally,
> Simply meant to be.

We found an outdoor bar and luckily found a table. This place was packed. Describing the setting would not do it justice. It was simply Spain. I admired a magnificent church that was right next to the bar. The four of us had the most pleasant conversation. Oscar, in his younger days, was a famous *fútbol* player in Spain. We call it soccer in the States. He played until he got injured, and then the following fourteen years, he was a soccer coach in the Canary Islands. Now he is an executive for some linen service in Madrid. He has been with Natalie for the past three years. They were so precious. Although not young, they portrayed a very young kind of love.

I shared with them my Texas background, and yes, I had to tell them we don't ride horses to work. I told them I was a passionate fisherman and how much I love to fish. I showed them a picture on my phone of my trophy fish, an 8'7" hammerhead shark I caught on my favorite fishing boat, *The Island Queen II*. They were in awe. They couldn't believe my catch. I told them about Sharkathon and how cool that tournament is. I explained it was a surf fishing contest on North Padre Island, one of the largest tournaments in Texas. They couldn't understand how anyone would have the guts to kayak bait out two to three hundred yards in shark-infested waters. Texans must be tough but crazy people. Gotta love 'em.

After a short dinner of mostly appetizers, we decided to go check out the church. I received my first stamp (*sello*) from a church. I had been obtaining my stamps for my passport, but mostly I was obtaining them at bars and of course at all the albergues I stayed at. Exploring the church was phenomenal. Upon making our way back to the albergue, we stopped on some steps, as Vance wanted to have a smoke. He rolled his own cigarettes, which I hadn't seen in quite some time. Before rolling it up, he pulled out a small square, and I watched as he chipped a few small pieces into his cigarette. I asked what it was, as I had never seen it before.

He causally replied, "Hash."

I suddenly got uncomfortable. Not to present myself as innocent when it comes to drugs, for I experienced several kinds in my younger days, but I hadn't touched the stuff in over thirty years. Amazingly, I never came across hash.

I responded naively, "Wow, I didn't know it was legal in Spain." He responded, "It's not."

Now I really felt uncomfortable, as we were out in public, and there was no effort to even try covering it up or hiding it. I was getting nervous. Oscar and Natalie reaffirmed it wasn't legal but that it wasn't a big deal in Spain. He lit up and enjoyed his little hash-infested cigarette.

> I wanted to dash
> When Vance pulled out the hash,
> But that would be rash.

I dashed anyway! They wanted to go to another bar, but I informed them that I was a little tired and my feet were starting to bother me, so I was heading back to the albergue. Truth was I wanted to get away from the drugs, and my feet truly were bothering me. I said good night and found my way back to the albergue.

This albergue had the smallest bathrooms of all that I stayed at. There were at least twenty women, and we had one shower and two sinks. I knew I would have to get up early to beat the crowd to the shower. I climbed into my bunk early that evening, wrote in my diary, Facebooked, said my prayers, and drifted off to a pleasant slumber.

CHAPTER 18

Day 6: August 27th, Santander to Santillana del Mar - 20.6 Miles

Put on the full armor of God, that you may be able to stand against the wiles of the devil.

—Ephesians 6:11

Walking through the city of Santander in the dark was actually quite enjoyable. I wasn't scared. I felt safe. I admired the flickering lights like stars plastered against the darkened skies. I passed Santa Cruz de Bezana and Boo de Piélagos. At Boo, yes a town name Boo, I had to catch a train to cross the river, as the only pedestrian bridge was nine kilometers away. My feet were beginning to become more painful, but I could still tolerate them. As the day progressed, the discomfort progressed with it. Perhaps it was because I pushed myself to walk 20.6 miles. I walked for a solid ten hours except that short but splendid train ride.

Of course, no surprise to me, I missed the station. When I began to question myself, a lovely couple was taking a walk, and I asked them if by chance I had missed it. Oh yes indeed, but they would walk me to it, as it was fairly close. They took me on a shortcut that passed their small but beautiful, colorful home. It was so cute I complimented its beauty and quaintness. They were so gracious to allow me to cut through the series of houses, as this was the shortcut to the station. I'm sure no other pilgrim had ventured this way off the common path, as it was private property and fenced.

They heard the train coming and instructed me to run to where it stops and not to bother buying the ticket from the machine because I wouldn't have time and I would certainly miss the train. They yelled to me as I was running toward the train not to worry because the conductor would come by, and I could pay him directly. That is, if he did come by.

It was to be a very short, two-kilometer train ride, so I stood right in front of the doors. The train stopped, but lo and behold, the doors did not slide open, and the blasted train started moving again! Heaven forbid, I missed my stop! What in the world was I to do? I totally freaked out. I turned to a gentleman standing next to me and asked him why the doors didn't open. He replied that I had to press the green button. Great, just great. I can speak Spanglish, but I certainly can't read Spanish. He said I could just get off at the next stop, which was Gornazo. I referred to my guidebook and felt reassurance when I saw the Camino right next to the tracks in Gornazo.

Joyfully, I jumped out this time, only to find no signs of the Camino. No arrows, no shells, no signs whatsoever. I crossed the tracks in hopes I was going the right direction when I saw an old man up on a nearby hill, waving me toward his direction and pointing down the road. I figured he knew I was a pilgrim and was helping me out. So I made my way in his direction. We conversed, and he asked me where I was from.

"Texas," I replied.

After our short conversation, as I was leaving, he tried to grab me and give me a kiss.

This little old nasty man pleaded, "Un besito?" (A little kiss?)

"Absolutely not!" I yanked myself away and yelled at him in Spanish, "Yo soy peregrina (I am a pilgrim), y la gente en este Camino (and people on this Camino) ayuda a los peregrinos (help pilgrims), y no hasten cosas como eso (and they don't do things like that). Ahora dime (Now tell me), es este el Camino correcto?" (is this the correct way for the Camino?).

My tone was angry, and I was literally yelling at him I was so upset.

He replied, "Si" (yes), and began apologizing.

I made it obvious how irate he made me as I stomped away. I thanked the Lord for helping me get out of that situation. I felt like the devil had thrown me a curve ball, but I was proud of myself for handling it the best way I knew how. Yelling!

I continued up the road and went quite a ways not seeing any signs for reassurance. I made it to Mar when I ran into a couple. They too were not feeling secure about being on the correct route. So the three of us walked together until we found a local store where a gentleman was just exiting. We asked him, and he gave us some relief by stating we were going the right direction. Thank you, Lord Jesus.

I made it past Requejada and Barreda before finally entering Santillana del Mar. Oh my, what an entrance it was. I felt like I had just stepped into a past century, medieval kind of town. My feet were truly hurting by the time I entered this magical kingdom. It was like a Harry Potter atmosphere. The cobblestone streets, the ancient buildings, the locals in their gothic and medieval attire. And the tourists? It was infested with tourists, everywhere. This was definitely a tourist town. I was absorbing every sight and sound I possibly could; it was so magnificent. My poor feet were so painful, but the sights were distracting me from the pain. The shops were so entertaining and charming. I couldn't help but visit a few.

I found the albergue, and upon entrance, it too captivated my senses. I had just stepped into the Munsters' very home. I absolutely love it! All this enchanting entertainment for a mere sixteen euros.

The gentleman who registered me actually escorted me to my dorm room. It was only for six pilgrims, so it was relatively small. I chose a lower bunk, unpacked, and showered. I noticed my feet, especially my ankles, were quite swollen and still very painful. I decided I better go look for a pharmacy and try to find some pain relief.

I really enjoyed the stroll through this gorgeous town and alas found the pharmacy. I asked for some ibuprofen and couldn't believe they charged me more than five euros for a mere twelve tablets. On top of that, they were only 400 mgs. I had spoken to my boyfriend, Jay, and he recommended maybe trying some athlete's tape and wrapping my ankles for support. Since my left foot was causing me more problems than the other, I wrapped that one. After leaving the pharmacy, I stopped at the corner bar and ordered a *patata* (potato and eggs, quiche-type pie) and a beer. I eagerly popped two of the pills into my mouth and guzzled it down with the great-tasting beer.

I had such a wonderful time sitting outside this delightful little bar, watching tourists walk by, taking pictures, yelling at their children, followed by more pictures and a lot more yelling. It was funny.

After visiting a few more stores and admiring their unique arts and crafts, I made my way back to the albergue in the early evening to call it a day due to my swollen, painful feet. Another pilgrim had checked in by the time I got back to my room, and he was in the process of unpacking on the bunk next to mine. I introduced myself. He told me his name was Karl and informed me he had been walking for approximately three months. He started his walk from his front door in Wren, Austria.

> An old man from Wren,
> Been walking since who knows when.
> With time he will win.

That is how the Camino trails started, pilgrims beginning their pilgrimage directly from their homes, and then they would walk back home. This absolutely amazed me. Most of us currently walk the one direction. Stop and think about multiplying that by two! He had walked across many countries before he even got to Spain. He was sixty-six years old and retired; he was taking his sweet time without an agenda. I was a bit envious. What I would give to have that luxury. Unfortunately, being limited with time, I was pushing my body to the brink and not realizing it. I was innocently unaware of any impending damage. His story kept me in awe with what he had encountered throughout his pilgrimage thus far. I could have sat there and listened to him all night. Sadly, because my feet were bothering me, I called it an early night, and by eight o'clock, I was bundled up in my sleeping bag, ready to drift into a much-needed restful night. I went through my usual nightly routine. I made a few phone calls, posted on Facebook, spoke to Jay one last time, and prayed.

Jay and I had a discussion regarding my feet. He told me either it was my will or my faith that was being tested. He encouraged me to stay strong in my faith and to remain hopeful. He encouraged me to rely on my Lord and my spirituality. I am so thankful that I have someone like Jay who not only believes in me but believes in God and encourages me in spiritual growth.

Was I being tested? If so, I would prove my faith in this endeavor. Therefore, I prayed and prayed hard until I prayed myself to sleep. *Lord God, please be with me.*

CHAPTER 19

Day 7: August 28th, Santillana del Mar to Comillas - 17.6 Miles

---

Not lagging in diligence, fervent in spirit, serving the Lord; rejoicing in hope, patient in tribulation, continuing steadfastly in prayer.

—Romans 12:11–12

I woke up with still painful feet, but certainly nothing that would prevent me from walking. A couple more pills ought to do the trick. I packed up and started walking out of this incredible fantasy town relatively early, as it would be greater than a fifteen-mile day.

There were churches galore today! Beautiful and enchanting churches. There were majestic and tiny churches. A red one, St. Peter ad Vincula, was a church in Cobreces that was gorgeous. A blue church was somewhere along this trail, but I just couldn't seem to find it. I wish I had the time to go into each and every one. If I'm ever as fortunate as Karl, I will return and do just that. And maybe fish a little too.

As I ventured a short distance to see one of these churches, I met a young blond-haired man by the name of Thomas from Slovakia.

When I introduced myself, he stated, "Oh you're Marissa! Ya, I heard about you!"

That caught me off guard! "What? What do you mean? What have you heard?"

He replied with this gorgeous smile and picture-perfect white teeth, "You're from Texas, right?"

"Absolutely," I replied.

People just naturally are intrigued with Texas. We chatted as we walked together to go check out that beautiful church.

> As he shared his smile,
> Thomas knew all the while
> These were magic miles.

My feet were really bothering me. They kept poking at the pain receptors that made their way to my brain. I had to slow down quite a bit because every step was beginning to be more and more challenging. As I approached Comillas, it was as enchanting and bewildering as Santillana del Mar was. Another gothic-looking section of town was filled with its townspeople, tourists, and pilgrims. Numerous outdoor restaurant seating areas filled the plaza. I had to walk through the middle of this activity to get to the albergue.

By the time I finally made it to the albergue, lo and behold, sitting on the all-pilgrim packed hillside was my non-believing friend, Neoneé. I had passed her earlier in the day as I was cutting across some cornfields. She had stopped under a tree and was having a picnic lunch. I stopped and conversed with her for a short while, and even though I left her sitting there eating her sandwich, she still beat me to the albergue. I never saw her pass me by. It may have been while I was visiting a church or bar for a break.

I was afraid I had lagged behind so much, mostly because of by blasted feet, that I wouldn't be able to attain a bunk. Sure enough, this albergue only had twenty bunks, and I appeared to be number twenty-one. Fortunately, by the grace of God, there were three cyclists in front of me, so I truly lucked out and would be allowed to bypass them according the albergue rules.

I laid my backpack in line and went back upon the hill and sat next to Neoneé to visit until the albergue opened. My feet were pounding the moment I sat down and relieved the pressure. I was afraid to take my boots off because I could feel my feet were quite swollen. I chatted with Neoneé and told her that I had read up on some of the spectacular buildings the architect, Antonio Gaudí, had designed in this town. I had planned to go visit some of these buildings after checking in, but my feet were talking to me by now. They were both angry with me and basically stated they would not have it. Therefore, I refrained and just admired what I could see from the albergue.

After I checked in and got stamped, I claimed my bunk up against the back wall. All the beds in this albergue were upstairs, while the kitchen area, washroom, and bathrooms were all downstairs. After unpacking, I washed up, got dressed, and put my sandals on instead of my boots. My feet were far too swollen and really quite painful, but I took a couple more ibuprofen, hoping the swelling would go down soon. I ventured back to the plaza, which was about a block or two away, to go have dinner with Neoneé, Thomas, and several other friends I had made along the way. They could tell I was having a hard time just by the way I was struggling to make it to the table.

I decided to diagnose myself with a left heel spur, as my left foot was ten times more painful than the right. After 17.6 miles in seven hours, I sat down with this wonderful group of people, again from all around the world, until I had to get back up on my dreadfully aching feet and make it back to the albergue. I practically crawled back, very slowly, and made it to my bunk in the early evening. My ankles were swollen, and the ache was relieved with a few more ibuprofen and elevating my feet. I thought for sure I just needed to rest these poor soles, and by morning, I would feel much better.

I felt somewhat awkward lying down in my bunk so early in the evening, like a grandmother or something. Oh yeah, I am one. I engaged in my nightly routine and kissed my sweet man good night via phone after I spent a great deal of time telling him about my feet. I Facebooked and then gently wandered into a moderately painful night, but I could handle it.

CHAPTER 20

Day 8: August 29th, Comillas to Serdio - 15.6 Miles

(The original plan was to make it to Columbres, 17.7 miles, but it didn't work out that way.)

But Jesus looked at them and said to them. "With men this is impossible, but with God all things are possible."
—Matthew 19:26

Prior to going to sleep last night, I set my alarm for 6:30 a.m., thirty minutes earlier than usual because I knew it would take me a little bit longer than normal to get to the bathroom, due to my aching feet. I felt that would give me plenty of time before all the other pilgrims started to stir. My internal alarm went off and woke me up just prior to my set alarm, so I turned it off. Even though I was going to walk slower today, I was still so excited to get started, and my feet felt better than the night before. So I immediately stood up to go to the bathroom and— oh my heavens!

My life flashed before my eyes. I suddenly felt like I had stepped on sharp knives that shot the most intense pain straight up both of my legs, to the point that I collapsed right back into my bed. I screamed in silence. My eyes widened like I had seen a ghost. I gasped and went into unexpected and sudden shock. *My Lord, my God, help me! What is happening?* I was no longer standing up, as I was in incredible pain. *Oh my dear God, oh my God, please, please help me.* I could not believe what was happening. *This isn't real; this just can't be. Lord, please.*

These few seconds of intolerable pain felt like an eternity. I was still. I dared not move. It was dark and quiet, and all the other pilgrims were still sound asleep. As my feet were bulging and pulsating, I began to cry in silence. I conjured up all the power I had in me, using every ounce of energy I could muster not to scream out loud as I lay there in astonishing agony. The tears began to flow, and then I realized I was not crying because I was in this incredible, unforgiving pain but because I suddenly realized I could not walk. I couldn't even stand up, much less walk. *Oh my heavens, my dearest Lord Jesus Christ, please help me.* I knew I could rely on my brain to help me handle and crush the pain, but the thought of not being able to walk was shattering my heart. I was emotionally breaking down in silence. The mental pain of knowing I could not walk was ten times more intense than this horrifying physical pain I was suddenly enduring. *I don't understand. Why is this happening? Lord, I need you. My dear Savior, please come help me.* All of this had to remain in darkened silence. I dared not wake these people. *This just can't be happening.* The tears were flowing uncontrollably.

I can't handle this. I simply can't wrap my head around this. Why, oh Lord? What on earth have I done? Oh please, dear Lord, please forgive me. All I want to do is walk. Jesus, where are you? I need you. I just want to walk.

The tears slowed down to a gentle stream as I lay there wondering what on earth I was to do. All I could do at that moment was pray. So I prayed, and I prayed, and I prayed. Shortly thereafter, I heard someone's alarm clock go off. I started hearing movement in the dorm and knew I had to deal with this situation. A phone light flickered across the room. Like mice, they began to stir. The tears continued to slow down but still found their way to my pillow. I needed to get a hold of myself. The pain was still there but had settled down to a brutal pounding, enough that I could manage to sit up on the side of the bed. The bilateral pulsations would not cease, but my courage would not wallow as I began mounting the pain like a horse. I would ride on my courage to help me stand. And I did. I stood. For a moment, I just stood. *I can and I will stand. Lord, please take my hand.*

With every slow movement I made, more and more pilgrims were awakening to greet the dawn of day. I feared pity at this point. I didn't want anyone to see what I was going through for fear of—well, I don't know of what but just for fear. I just didn't want anyone feeling sorry for me. I sat there frozen in time as I watched others getting ready for the adventures of the day. I could not hide my grief. I was in pain I was trying so hard to hide, but that was just unrealistic. It was practically painted on my forehead. "Can't walk."

At this point, I had no choice but to stand and try to walk. By now, my bladder was screaming for relief. I had to get to the bathroom, pain or no pain. I had no choice. My mind was confused, my heart was broken, my feet were dying, and now my bladder wanted to take center stage. *Oh, dear Lord God, help me through this.*

I took my first step as I grabbed a bed post. Those invisible knives were there. Oh how utterly painful, but I had to. I would not give up. *I can and will take that next step.* I grabbed a pole and took a step. I grabbed the next bed and took a step. The wall, a step. I eventually made it to the stairs as the hurried pilgrims were walking right past me, or around me, passing rapidly, scurrying down the stairs. I looked down upon this dreadful, evenly descending stairwell. *Oh my dearest God, please I beg of you, please guide me down as easily as possible. Please help me make it to the bathroom. I so desperately need your help right now.* My poor bladder was about ready to burst.

The stairwell had cleared of pilgrims running up and down, so now was my chance to accept this challenge, and I did. One step. *Oh my God, help me.* Another. *Jesus, please. I can and will do this with you, Jesus, by my side, for it is in his power that I will succeed in descending these horrendous never-ending stairs.* And alas, I did it! I reached the bottom! *Oh, thank you, my sweet Lord.* Now to make it to the throne, which was just a few more feet away. Holding on to walls and whatever I could grab helped me make it. *Thank you, oh Lord, my heavenly Father.* I made it. Ah yes, relief, but unfortunately, it was only my bladder that was relieved. The rest of my body was shattered and crumbled. *I can and will do this with the help of my sweet Savior. Please, Lord, help me.* I made it one slow and painful step at a time, holding on to whatever I could reach, and I made it to the sink to wash up. As refreshing as the cool water and toothpaste was, it provided not even a fraction of relief to my poor failing feet.

What could this possibly be? I just can't understand it. I looked in the mirror, and my bloodshot, teary eyes stared back. So I closed them and prayed. *Please, dear Lord, please help me make it back upstairs.* The thought of those piercing knives awaiting every step I had to take was devastating. *I can't do this without you, God. Please help me manage this.* And so I proceeded back up the stairs and to my bunk in deep and concentrated prayer.

It was quite obvious something was terribly wrong with me as I took one painful step after another. Pilgrims would stop and ask if they could help me out or do something for me.

I painted that fake smile on my face and replied, "No, no thank you. I'll make it."

When I finally reached my bunk, I sat down, dazed at all the rapid movements in the room of pilgrims getting ready to leave. The packing up, the unwrapping of a breakfast bar, the zipping of a sleeping bag, the foreign conversations, the busyness of the room saddened me greatly because I could not be a part of it. I sat there absorbing my pounding, incredible pain. A tear I had fought so hard to hold back found its way down my cheek. I couldn't understand. I was so lost. All I wanted to do was walk, but I knew I couldn't, and it was devastating.

Julie, an acquaintance from Germany, walked to my bed, sat next to me, and put her arm around my shoulders. That's all it took. Now that stream of tears was like a flood gate had just opened up, and they flowed uncontrollably. I started crying so hard I couldn't even talk for a moment.

"Sweetie," she said, "this is a sign. You have to get help. Something is wrong, and it's God's way of telling you that you can't do this anymore. It's time to go home."

Excuse me? What did she say? No, I could not comprehend those words. They would not filter through my thought process. They just jumbled in my mind.

"I just wanna walk," I pleaded.

Please, God, please be with me. Please help me do this. Please give me strength.

"Tell you what. Go ahead and pack up, and I'll help you to the bus stop," Julie offered.

She was being as kind as she possibly could, and I greatly appreciated her sincere concern. I took a deep breath, got the tears under control, and started packing up my belongings while sitting on the side of the bed. My sleeping bag was extremely difficult to get into its tiny bag. I continued tearing up and praying. I was having the most difficult time trying to accept the fact that I could not walk anymore. I continued praying during the entire packing process. I was so incredibly sad, thinking that I was going to have to fly home today. My plan, my dream, my goals were shattered.

Reluctantly, I continued packing, as I didn't want to hold up Julie from starting her walk. As I was almost finished, Thomas approached my bed and said he would help me too. He took my backpack in one arm and had his backpack on his back. He said he would help me along with Julie to the bus stop. My bloodshot eyes looked up to his sculptured, perfect features and blond hair, and I thanked him. Both Thomas and Julie supported me, one on each side, and assisted me down those dreadful stairs.

Once we had made it down to the bottom, we entered the small patio. To the left side, there were several old walking sticks lying against the wall, left by previous pilgrims. Thomas grabbed two of them and handed them to me. He said these would help me get a little pressure off of my feet. Old sticks that apparently had been used by former pilgrims to help them make it to Columbres. *Now, they are supposed to assist me to make it to a bus stop where a bus is supposed take me to an airport where I'm supposed to jump into a plane that is supposed to take me home. Supposedly.* There they came again, those stinking tears. I took the old walking sticks and used them as crutches to relieve some pressure. It was the slightest bit of help, but at that moment, anything would help. Regardless, each step was like stepping on a sharp knife over and over and over.

Even with the help of my two angel friends and my sticks, I hurt so terribly bad. A few blocks away, there was a simple bus stop. Just a cover with the plexiglass on three sides and a bench. It was empty and appeared more like a small, abandoned shelter with a solitary bench waiting for me. Upon arrival, my two sweet friends sat me down as gently as they could. I would have never made it that far without their help. *Thank you, Lord, for sending me these angels.* Thomas laid my backpack next to me, and both took turns giving me hugs. Thomas instructed that when a bus came, to simply tell the driver that I needed to get to an airport, and they could provide me with further instructions.

"They'll give you all the directions you need. Just get to the airport and get home safely. You really need to take care of yourself," instructed my friend.

I nodded in agreement. Although I understood, I couldn't comprehend what was taking place. "Yes, yes, thank you. Thank you so much for all your help. I'm so sorry I have held you up."

"No, no, no. I'm glad I could help," replied Thomas.

Julie too expressed her willingness to help a pilgrim in need.

God sent these two beautiful angels to help me make it out of the albergue and to a place where I could figure things out. They sadly left me with great pity in their expressions as they said their goodbyes.

"Farewell, Miss Texas! And good luck!"

"God be with you guys! Thanks for everything," I replied.

As their silhouettes disappeared in the misty gray morning, I looked around. This place was so solemn, so peaceful, so beautiful. My feet were still pounding, and I was just as upset with them as they were with me. Why was it so quiet? There were no cars, no people, no activity other than the birds singing their praises. Such beauty, and yet I was overcome with sadness. I sat and waited for that bus for five, ten, fifteen minutes, and nothing. The entire time, all I could do was pray. Twenty minutes passed, and still nothing. Every minute was digging me into a deeper hole of despair. What was I going to do? The only thing I could hang on to right then was prayer. I had hit the bottom of my despair and confusion of not knowing what to do. *Dear Lord, please I beg of you, please help me figure this out. Please help me walk. All I want to do is walk. Such a simple task, and I can't do it without you. Please, please be with me. You are my only hope. I just want to walk.* I prayed so hard, consistently, nonstop. *I just want to walk, God. Please, I beg of you, I need you so bad.* I have so much faith in my Lord Jesus. I handed him my all, for I was entirely in his hands. There was no bus, there were no people, and had it not been for my faith in the holy Lord, there would be no hope. But I have a great and powerful faith in my Lord, my faithful Jesus Christ, the spirit of the Almighty. And therefore I would continue praying.

It finally dawned on me that no bus was going to come my way, and even if it did, it could not take me to an airport. I was in a small tourist-type town, and this silly bus stop was probably just for local transportation, if it even had a public transportation system. There was no way I was going to get to an airport. This was hopeless.

I asked God to take me in his hands, as I had made the decision to attempt to walk. I stood up, and the pain had not eased up at all. It was intense, but I had built up an unsurpassed level of determination and will and found the courage with God's assistance to place one foot in front of the other. And so I did. My backpack was reloaded to my able back, and the two wasted, spattered walking sticks were held tightly within my grip.

One intense step, one pause. Another painful step, pause. Again a flaming step, pause, followed by another, pause. The steps continued one by one. My prayers continued. *Please, God, be with me. Please help me do this.* As the steps continued, the pauses shortened with each step. The pain slowly began to ease, and every next step was just a tiny bit easier than the last. I continued placing one foot in front of the other as these elderly crutches assisted in easing the weight inflicted with each step. And I continued praying and stepping and praying and stepping and stepping and praying and walking and praying, and I couldn't stop. It just kept happening. *What's going on? I don't understand.* The pain was lessening more and more with each step and each prayer. Suddenly, before I knew it, I was walking. I was walking, and the pain had decreased tremendously. I began walking faster and faster, and *I was walking!* *Oh, my heavenly Father, I am walking!* It was like there were wings upon my back. I felt lifted. I couldn't believe what was happening. I was actually walking! Out of nowhere, I was walking at my normal pace, and I could tolerate it. I was so amazed and baffled I pulled out Jay's GoPro camera and started videotaping myself because I was experiencing a miracle. I started bawling because I was walking. I couldn't believe it! I cried and cried and cried, and I thanked my Lord. "Thank you, God, thank you! Thank you for helping me do this." I still couldn't believe I was actually walking. After about three hundred yards, I felt secure enough to actually leave one of the sticks against a tree, in hopes it would help another pilgrim in need, sometime in the future. I was experiencing an absolute miracle. I was walking!

I started out the day crying because I couldn't walk, and now I found myself crying because I could! My tears had turned to smiles and then laughter. I felt like I was being carried. I was so elated that I could continue on this journey that I was so determined to complete. I knew that my only hope, the only solution was to rely on my faith in my God and savior, Jesus Christ. And so be it, I walked, with minimal pain and a smile. I walked and prayed, prayed and walked in joyful, miraculous harmony.

I had popped two more 400 mg tablets of ibuprofen that morning before I attempted to get up and walk with Thomas and Julie, so I knew I could take two more every six hours. Problem was those were my last two, and I knew I would need some soon for the swelling. As I continued to walk, the pain slowly and gradually started to increase. I continued walking several miles, and as I was entering the next city, San Vicente de la Barquera, I had to cross a lengthy and very busy bridge. The path for pedestrians was somewhat narrow, so since I was walking relatively slowly, I tried to stay on the far right side so that people could pass me by. As they did, it felt like sprinters in a race, and I was the lone turtle. The busyness of the city got louder as I approached its crowded sidewalks. Suddenly I was in the midst of an extremely busy city. My feet were talking to me, telling me I better get them some relief fairly soon, or I may end up in another devastating situation. Therefore, I ventured off the beaten path into the lively, rumbling business district to find a much-needed pharmacy. I had walked a good two or three blocks before I saw what appeared to be a grocery store. I could ask for directions and buy some fresh fruit to refuel my energy. I began limping again, for the aching was increasing along with the swelling of my ankles. I asked the kind lady at the checkout where I could locate the nearest pharmacy.

She responded with a smile, "Just a couple more blocks to the left. Then take a right, and you will see a green pharmacy sign."

Simple enough. I graciously thanked her for her kindness and left the store. Right outside at the entrance to this grocery store was some seating that surrounded a tree with some flowers and shrubs. I sat down to quickly eat an apple and have a drink of soda water. It felt good to relieve my poor, aching feet for just a few minutes as well. I got up and started walking in the direction that sweet lady instructed me to, and as I turned the second corner and saw the pharmacy sign, it was like the emerald city of Oz awaiting my arrival. What a beautiful sign.

I limped into this tiny building and approached the counter. It didn't take long before a young lad was waiting on me. He kindly asked me what he could get for me, and I asked him if he had any ibuprofen. He followed with questioning me what strength I was looking for. In Spanish, I asked him what my options were. He replied several options, but when I heard 600 mg, my eyes enlarged, and my ears stood up.

I repeated, "Six hundred? I can buy that over the counter?"

"Of course," he answered.

"How much?" I asked, and when he said forty tablets for two euros, I couldn't believe my ears.

Are you kidding me? Jackpot!

"Oh my! Yes, I'll take two boxes." I thought, *That should last me a good while.*

I thought back for a second while he was ringing up my total of the pharmacy in Santillana Del Mar, the touristy town. I thought about how deeply I had been gauged monetarily; now I realized how badly. As soon as I completed my purchase, I took two tabs immediately and then packed both boxes into my backpack before exiting this lifesaving pharmacy.

I stepped back out into the Time Square type of atmosphere this city was offering. I turned toward the direction I had come to backtrack and return to the Camino where I had left off. Just as I was turning the corner, I caught a glimpse from an elderly gentleman who was walking across the street toward me. We made eye contact for less than a split second, but I immediately noticed the cane he had clutched in his wrinkled hand. It was shaped like the wings of a bird in flight. It captured my attention. I immediately turned left to trace those necessary extra steps down the five, possibly six, blocks I had walked just to find the pharmacy.

My feet were truly aching now. The pain had gradually increased with each passing mile. As I continued walking down this crowded sidewalk, the first block or two, I sensed I was being followed. The aura got more intense as I continued. I was still using that one last stick I had taken from the last albergue, and it was helping to a small degree. With increasing discomfort and the thought that someone was stalking me, I was nervous. It was really getting bothersome. I just felt strongly that I was being followed. Was it that old silver-haired man I witnessed crossing the street? I wasn't sure, but my intuition was knocking hard on my brain, saying, "Yes, someone is following you." I was walking past a general store or maybe a barbershop. There were two old men sitting outside, and after I passed them, I could hear them greet this individual that I believed was following me. My intuition was correct. Someone had indeed been following me, but why? I dared not turn around.

When he responded to the two old men, "Hola compadres," it was confirmed. It was that old man. He was following me. Why? I was getting nervous and confused. I had just passed block four or five and was getting closer to returning to where I needed to be. I was just about half a block from resuming my Camino when this old man passed me by and turned around. I was right; he had been following me since I left the pharmacy. He turned around and stopped me in my tracks. I was startled and scared as he asked, "Hablas Espanol?" (Do you speak Spanish?)

I immediately responded, "Si, si entiendo." (Yes, yes I understand.)

He commanded, "Espedate aqui." (Wait right here.)

That I certainly didn't understand. I knew what he said, but I didn't understand why, so I informed him, "Eso, señor, no entiendo." (That, sir, I do not understand.)

"Si, si entiendes. (Yes, yes you do.) Espedate aqui." (Wait, wait right here.) *Heavenly Jesus, please be with me. What is going on? I don't understand why this complete stranger, this little old man, would tell me to stand still and not move.* As I was pondering in my frozen confusion, he walked across the street and entered a green door into a building. *Dear Lord, please watch over me. I am so confused. What is going on?* Within a few seconds, this little old man who had been stalking me for the last four or five blocks came back out of that green door with what appeared to be polished, expensive-looking walking sticks. It crossed my mind for a moment he might be trying to sell me these expensive canes, so immediately I knew I would have to refuse. I noticed as he was walking back across the street toward me that he wasn't using his own cane, and as he got closer, I noticed they were walking sticks. The kind they sell to pilgrims along the many trails. He was cutting the tape that was holding these two beautiful polished canes together as he walked closer to me.

He approached me, and I immediately said, "Aye no, no señor, muy caro, no, no tengo dinero para eso." (Oh no, no, sir, very expensive, no, I don't have money for that.) I was shaking my head in a "no" manner all the while, and still he aggressively kept approaching me with a controlling attitude, cutting the last piece of tape, ignoring my refusing remarks.

He had just finished cutting that last piece of tape when he said, "No, regalo." (No, gift.)

He shoved the two gorgeous, immaculately polished walking sticks into my hands as he took my old one from me. I was stunned and shocked. I didn't know how to respond other than to look up to the sky and thank my good Lord.

"Thank you. Thank you, God." My eyes started getting watery, and my voice was shaky. I didn't want to break down in front of this old, gracious, heavenly sent man who only a few moments ago I had misjudged as a stalker. *Please, dear Lord, forgive me.*

All I could do at this sudden, unexpected, miraculous moment was say, "Gracias, muchisimas gracias señor," (Thank you, thank you so very much, sir), before I started breaking down. I turned around and started back to the Camino before he could witness me breaking down in my emotional state of mind.

He smiled as I was turning around and yelled out to me, "Buen Camino!"

Sure enough, the tears just came streaming down my face. I started bawling like a baby. I didn't realize that he had grabbed my old walking stick before he handed me the replacements. They were much larger and longer than the old one. They were finely polished, and the handles were wrapped with leather and gold button tacks. The hand grips even had the little rope loops to go around your hands with tassels so that you didn't drop them. The tips of these miraculous, heaven-sent crutches were covered with steel points so that they would not fray and therefore would last a long time. The name of the town, S. Vte de la Barquera, was engraved down the sides of each stick.

I was so amazed as I continued crying and walking. With one foot in front of the other, the tears also continued one after the other. The experience virtually took so much pain away from my ailing feet.

I couldn't believe I was not in the severe agony I had been in earlier. Yes, perhaps the ibuprofen was kicking in, but I strongly believe the miracle I had just experienced relieved a tremendous amount of pain. I looked up to the sky and thanked my dear Lord again and again and again. I was so amazed and so bewildered when I realized it was through my great faith in his power and gracious mercy that I had been delivered these spiritual crutches by one of his many angels.

"Thank you, God. Thank you, thank you, thank you." The tears flowed as I humbly limped away from this spectacular town. San Vicente de la Barquera, I will never ever forget you. My mysterious, elderly, stalking angel, I will never forget you. Miracle number two for the day had just taken place.

Regardless of the pain, my load had just been lightened. Yes, literally to my feet, but my hope, my determination, and my perseverance had just been refueled by the power of my Almighty God. I can't thank you enough, Lord Jesus. I will serve you every day of my life. I promise. Thank you.

And I continued my walk. *How anyone can believe there is no God is beyond me*, I kept thinking. *He has made me an instrument of his testimony. I am living proof. Miracles are not coincidences. There is a difference. Not only have I seen them, I have just experienced them firsthand.* I couldn't comprehend this amazement I had just experienced. After about half a mile, I stopped and laid my new crutches aside so I could take a picture of them and share them with my sister on Facebook. Since day one, at the airport, I had ended every day with a posting of my day's accomplishment for my dearest sister, Thelma. I wanted her to know immediately of the miracles I had encountered thus far today. I just couldn't wait until the end of the day. It was still unbelievable. I didn't know if anyone would question these miracles. *Not if they are believers*, I told myself.

I had ibuprofen on board, I had new crutches, and I had renewed hope. The pain had nothing on my elation of this entire encounter. I continued my unbelievable journey and made it all the way to

Serdio, which was a full 11.8 miles! I couldn't believe it! A day that started out with an inability to stand to a miraculous 11.8 miles of walking! Wow! As amazing as I felt this day, I knew it was my faith in Jesus Christ that was carrying me. I felt it physically, mentally, emotionally, and most importantly, spiritually. I prayed and thanked him with every step. Occasionally, when I wasn't sure I was going the right direction, I would pray and ask God to show me a sign.

"Please, dear Lord, show me the next arrow." It never failed; within seconds, an arrow or a shell or a sign would appear. Just as would my smile. Thank you, God. For I relied on my faith, and with that alone, the next step could be taken.

When I entered Serdio, I stopped at the first bar I encountered for a quick bathroom break and to eat. I ordered, no surprise here, Menu del Dia. As I was enjoying my meal, Thomas entered the bar with another gentleman. When he caught a glance of me at the table, his eyes widened in astonishment, and his mouth dropped.

He came running up to me and excitedly yelled, "Oh my goodness, Marissa! I can't believe it! How in the world?" He couldn't even finish his sentence he was so amazed.

"Wow, just wow! Dave, this is the girl I was telling you about. Did you actually walk here?" questioned Thomas.

"Please join me," I replied. "I gotta tell you the details. Absolute miracles today, my friend!"

He introduced me to his new friend, Dave. Dave was from Canada, probably in his late forties or early fifties, slightly younger than I. He was bald, and he was carrying a guitar on his back, so I already liked him.

"I heard about you. Can't wait to hear your story," said Dave as he leaned toward me to shake my hand.

They sat down at my table and ordered a beer. I, needless to say, ordered a second.

I started right off where Thomas and Julie had left me, at the bus stop. The fact that no bus ever came was surprising to Thomas. I told them both that I just started praying and praying and just putting my entire belief in God and my faith in his existence to help me do what I could not do on my own. I told them how I got rid of one of the old sticks when I started walking at a rapid pace and how I felt like I was being carried. I told them about the trip to the pharmacy and the old man who was stalking me. I shared with them the miraculous crutches presented to me, and they grabbed them and admired their beauty like they were Michelangelo sculptures. They were in awe.

"Wow, incredible. I'm amazed. I thought for sure your trip was over and I'd never see you again," said Thomas.

I replied that God had everything to do with it and through him all thing were possible.

The three of us got to know each other much better. We sat there for the next couple hours just sharing stories with each other. Dave showed me pictures of his two sons. They were only about two years apart, but they were polar opposites. He explained how the oldest was all into smoking dope and chilling. His younger son, totally the opposite, was so into his studies and constantly trying to plan his future and save money, things like that. The oldest was filthy and didn't clean up after himself, while the other was just the opposite. It's funny because I have my two older daughters, and I could relate. I greatly appreciated when Dave said, "Regardless of their differences, I love them both the same."

So many people, parents, probably have the same story when comparing their children. I thoroughly enjoyed his story and pictures. I shared my hammerhead shark picture and that story and told them about my work and my family, and they continued sharing theirs with me. Thomas, still single, was still so young. He was working on his story. What I envied about Thomas was that he was experiencing travel and other cultures at such a young age, whereas, here I was, at fifty-five.

Thomas informed me that they were staying in Sergio for the night. My feet were starting to talk to me and pulsate, so I knew I couldn't make it another six miles as originally planned. Therefore, it didn't take but a second to conclude that I needed to change my itinerary for the first time and stay in Serdio. Thomas and Dave gave me directions to the albergue. They said they were coming back to hang out and invited me to join them if I was up to it. They didn't have to ask twice. I was excited to hang out with my new friends even if my feet were hurting, and indeed they were, but I could certainly handle it.

Obviously, by now it was time for some more ibuprofen. The albergue was a few dreadful blocks away, but again, with faith and trust in my Lord, I made it. I purchased my bunk, set up my bed, and showered prior to returning to the bar. This entire process took three times longer than for the average pilgrim, but I just couldn't rush. I knew I was already pushing my poor feet to their brink for the day. So I took my sweet time. While I was getting dressed and slipping my feet into my sandals, I noticed how swollen they were, and I apologized to them as though they were individuals with their own life and personalities. I apologized for putting them through this agony but pleaded with them to please bear with me and help me accomplish this mission. I finished getting dressed and started back to the bar. With the Lord holding my hand, I made it.

They were already sitting down at one of the outside tables with another pilgrim, a very friendly female, but for the life of me, I could not remember her name. While we were chatting and drinking this most appreciated adult beverage, I noticed a middle-aged gentleman sitting with three other men at a table next to us. He kept staring at me. After about the third time of my catching him staring at me, he finally got up and started walking toward me.

"Hola, con permiso." (Hello, with permission.)

"Si?" (Yes?) I replied.

"Te vi caminando con mucho dolor," he continued. (I saw you walking with a lot of pain.)

"Si, si senor, mis pies me estan causando muchos problemas." (Yes, yes, sir. My feet are giving me much trouble.)

He responded by explaining, "Juego mucho futból, y hay

momentos en que mis pies me dan mucho dolor." (I play a lot of soccer, and there are times when my feet give me a lot of pain.) He continued with, "Tengo una crema que me ayuda mucho. Si te la traigo, si la usaras?" (I have a cream that helps me a lot. If I bring it to you, will you use it?)

Oh my heavenly Father, where did this stranger come from? I couldn't believe out of nowhere, this sweet, sweet soul just popped up and asked to help me. How incredibly thoughtful, how kind, how sweet.

"Si, si señor. Muchisimas gracias." (Yes, yes sir. Thank you so very much.)

With that being said, he scrambled off to his home, which must have been very nearby, for he only took a couple of minutes to return. When he got back to my table, he handed me a tube of cream as he explained that it was an anti-inflammatory type of cream. Both of my ankles were a good two to three plus edema. I applied it to both of my ankles as he continued talking. The powerful scent reminded me of Bengay. I finished and handed the tube back to him, but he told me to keep the remainder of the tube because he had another at home. He wanted me to have it for the rest of my trip. How kind and sweet of this stranger. I just couldn't thank him enough; I greatly appreciated his kindness.

"Dios te bendiga." (God bless you), I told him sincerely.

"Buen Camino," he replied as he walked back to his table.

I simply smiled without effort and thanked him again for his extreme kindness.

I turned to my friends and said, "God is so good. That's the fourth time he has sent me an angel in one day." My blessings have been endless.

"I totally agree, God is good. I'm so thankful he is watching over you," said Thomas.

I had a lovely visit with my friends, and the pain had diminished greatly, but once I stood up on my feet, the pain slowly crept up again.

I told everyone, "Buenas noches. Nos vemos en la mañana."

(Good night. See you in the morning.) And my heaven-sent crutches carried me back to the albergue.

After sorting all my belongings and cocooning in my sleeping bag, it didn't take long for me to slip into some very deep, engaging thoughts about the realism of God and his goodness. I went through my nightly routine, but tonight was different. It was filled with miracles. I couldn't tell enough of my story in such short amount of time. I shared what I could on FB. It was so difficult to refrain from all the details. In general, I just said today was one of the most miraculous days of my life. Believe me, I can't explain in detail here either, but just take my word for it, it was miraculous. They had already seen the crutches, so I knew they, whoever they were, besides my sister, knew I had experienced very special miracles God had sent my way.

Thank you, my dearest Jesus Christ. Thank you for walking beside me and helping me accomplish the unbelievable feats of today. I couldn't have done it without you. This is the base of faith, for without faith, there can be no spiritual miracles. For through Him all things are possible.

Miracles Abundant

Of this I do believe: they are sent from up above,
Of faith, oh hope, of love.
With Him I will achieve everything that's meant to be,
Of us, of you, of me.
A day does not go by, while my eyes are opened wide,
As these miracles abundant do not hide.
I will not question why, as He delivers them to me,
For with these I can clearly see
That next to me He walks, placing wings upon my back.
My pure faith I will not lack.
How fortunate our talks, for I am here to say,
Blessed He throws miracles my way.

CHAPTER 21

Day 9: August 30th, Serdio to Andrin - 25.7 Miles

(The original plan was Colombres to Llanes. Dream on!)

I thank my God always concerning you for the grace of God which was given to you by Christ Jesus, that you were enriched in everything by him in all utterance and all knowledge, even as the testimony of Christ was confirmed in you, so that you come short in no gift, eagerly waiting for the revelation of our Lord Jesus Christ.

—Corinthians 1:4–7

Today I was supposed to enjoy 14.6 miles of the beauty of Spain, but since I didn't make it to Colombres, I had to make up 6.8 miles I had lost. This is where I went wrong. I believed my walking sticks, my ice, the cream, and ibuprofen would help me handle the pain, allowing me to catch up to my previously planned itinerary. Therefore, I was looking at a good twenty-one miles. It was my idiotic determination getting in the way of rational thinking. I walked, and I prayed, looking for my signs, my shells, and my arrows. I was handling it quite well and thanking the good Lord for being with me and guiding me at every turn; with every step, he was there. I passed Colombres, followed by Pan Dulces, and all the precious little towns and villages in between, kissing my cross and looking up to the skies, making that constant spiritual connection.

Rain made its presence known. I was prepared though through the blessings of my dear friends Henry and Andrea, who gifted me with that rain poncho specifically for this trip. I enjoyed laughter as I remembered trying to convince them that I was going on this adventure. *God, thank you for blessing my life with those two.* The rain was sporadic but never really pounded down on me. Quietly, it lifted and casually would return for a short hello.

Today was another coastal-viewing hiking day. Truly my favorite with its endless beauty. *Lord, I cannot get enough of your creation. Thank you for blessing me with this incredible opportunity to experience a mere fraction of your enchanting creation.* At one point, I encountered several fences that I had to climb over into private property. This confused me a bit, while at the same time it fascinated me that the owners would allow so many pilgrims to enter their coastal acreage to continue their travels to Santiago.

All these handmade makeshift ladders were so awesome, so unique, and so purposeful. I greatly appreciated them as I made my way over several barbwire fences. My feet were tolerable though painful, and I was able to pull myself up and over into the next stunning view. Grazing pastures lined the timeless, carved stone cliffs overlooking the blue waters on the Bay of Biscay. This is what my heart ached for. This endless beauty. I began following a trail into this solemn land, and then suddenly it became uncomfortable. Up ahead were several cattle doing exactly what cattle are supposed to be doing. Grazing. I could not shrug off this uncomfortable feeling you get when you're intimidated by something much larger and stronger than you. An intimidating fear of a large object you have absolutely no control over and its possible dangerous actions.

Oh dear Lord, how I need you right now. Please protect me, please help me, please be with me. Oh my dear Savior, here we go.

Okay, I managed to pass one. Thank you, Lord. "Don't make eye contact," I told myself. *Oh dear God, hold me close. There goes another.* My heart was beating a bit faster than normal. *Help me, Lord. Please be with me. Oh heaven, I'm nervous.* That doubled when I saw a few yards ahead there was a baby calf. *Which one is the mama cow? Oh dear Lord, don't leave me. I desperately need you.* That baby calf was inches from the trail I was walking on, and I had to pass right by her. *Please, mama cow, I won't touch her. I promise.*

With all my faith, I was able to pass right by mama and baby cow without a glitch. I sighed with relief until I turned and there were two more huge cows standing right on my trail while munching down on grass. *Here we go again. Lord, please carry me. Get me through this, please, Jesus.* The situation was a bit different and much more challenging. You see, I couldn't walk around these beasts because the trail was right next to a cliff's edge. I could walk behind them, but I disregarded that idea for fear they might consider a swift kick. I don't know cows. I don't trust cows, and I don't know how they think. I don't know if they even know how to think. I wasn't taking any chances. I decided to try something different. Perhaps they understood a little English. I started talking to them gently in a kind and tender voice.

"Come on, sweetie, you have this entire hill and slope to graze on, and all I get is this skinny little trail, so go on now. Get out of my way. Go on, Elsie, Bessie, Betty, or whatever your names are. Just get out of my way."

Lo and behold! They listened!

Oh thank you, Jesus! They simply complied, and I went on my merry way. Really? Did that just happen? I was stunned. These fellas just listened and moved out of my way. I couldn't believe it! As soon as I climbed the next fence, I felt a great deal of relief. I thanked the Lord for watching over me and was so very happy that this cow encounter had gone smoothly. *Thank you, Jesus.*

My beautiful walking sticks helped carry me past the Bufones De Arenilla, an impressive geological feature. Cracks have formed within the rock cliffs, allowing for eruptions of seawater as high as twenty meters when the waves are strong. It was another pilgrim I had just recently passed that told me it was a fascinating site and one I shouldn't miss. I thanked him kindly and accepted the recommendation. As I got closer to the holes opening, it was getting more and more dangerous with the uneven rocks and sharp edges. I grabbed my polished poles, and they protected me from slipping or falling. Unfortunately, the waves were not strong enough to elevate or spit the water up the holes in the cliffs, but I could certainly hear all the anger of the water down below. It was truly scary. I absorbed as much beauty as my mind could engulf but knew I couldn't stay long, waiting for the waves' power to strengthen. With the constant twisting and balancing act I was trying to carry out with my poor feet, they responded with a pain level creeping up on me faster than I cared for. I sensed my overall body was getting generally fatigued, not just my feet. I was still a fair distance from my day's destination. I had re-planned for it to end in Adrin. My faithful guidebook instructed me that there was a hotel named La Casona de Adrin (The Big House of Adrin). In order to get there, I would have to follow the footpath for 3.4 km. It joined a paved road that would eventually land me in Adrin.

Thinking I was on the right path, as I continued seeing my arrows, the path led me to an area where more and more people were appearing. I somehow had entered a wooded area, which confused me because I didn't recall any of this in my book, so I wasn't sure where I actually was. I observed families, children, couples, and even lone hikers up and down these trails. It appeared to be some sort of natural park. Following a couple for a short distance, I suddenly found myself entering a cave. *Where am I? There is no mention of a cave in my guidebook, so now I'm really confused.*

At the entrance to the cave, I turned around, knowing I had gone the wrong way, and before entering inside, a little girl probably nine or ten years old was exiting, with her family not far behind. I asked her if there was a path that went through the cave, and she informed me it was only a cave with no other exit. *Duh, Marissa, what do you think a cave is?* She read the disappointment on my face as I thanked her for her time.

It was a beautiful cave, and I wish I had the time to go explore just as all these vacationers were doing, but I was just a lost pilgrim. Therefore, I had to backtrack to where I saw my last arrow and try to figure something out from there. *Oh, dear Lord, here I go again. Please help me.* My feet were really starting to hurt, so I popped my pills and gulped them down. I figured I would follow a few people and eventually find an exit out of this park. Somehow I managed to escape the hidden woods and caves, feeling like I was in a cartoon. I walked through the parking lot and saw the same little nine-year-old girl with her family, getting into their car. I stopped and asked her father directions to Adrin. He pointed and gave me instructions and reassured me it wasn't too far. *Honey, even ten feet on these excruciating, swollen, and painful feet is far.* I kept that thought to myself. I noticed the child couldn't take her eyes off of me the entire time I was conversing with her dad. She must have found me intriguing. Could it have been my Spanglish? I thanked him and the little girl for their time and continued on.

I kept walking in the direction as instructed by this sweet family, thanking the Lord for sending them my way. My painful search for Adrin continued as I followed the road that brought me to a fork. My choices were either straight along a fence line or to the right down a hill where I couldn't see too far due to the road taking a steep curve. Which shall it be? I went straight down the fence line for about thirty yards and suddenly felt uneasy. I prayed and begged God to direct me the right way. At this point, I simply didn't feel right. *Please, Lord, show me the way.* I turned around, went back to the fork, and took the downhill route around the curve. My blessed walking sticks helped me tremendously going downhill. They relieved a great deal of pressure from my heels with each step.

It was just so much worse going downhill on my feet. All I could do was continue praying because nothing I was passing by had been referenced in my guidebook. I was out there alone on the road—no cars, no pilgrims, no people of any sort, just the road, the hills, and the sun starting to go down. At one point, I was beginning to feel hopeless because today's venture just wouldn't end, and I was really hurting by now. I had never hiked this many hours in one day, even while training. God and I had a very long and serious conversation. I had so much faith in his being and his mercy. I simply could do no more than believe that he would guide me, carry me, and take me to where I needed to go. So I kept walking and praying.

After continued and constant prayer, I approached this quaint little town just after 7:00 p.m. I desperately needed some rest. I was aching so badly. I asked a local for directions to La Casona (The Big House), but when I got there, no one would answer the blasted door. It was just that—a big huge house with a big huge door and a big huge doorbell that no one would answer. Just great. I was anxious and desperate, so I didn't give up that easily. After knocking and ringing aggressively, finally someone came to the front door after about ten minutes. A lady gently opened the massive door to the massively huge house. She informed me that there were no rooms available. *What? Are you kidding me?* I couldn't believe my ears. My feet couldn't believe my ears. *Oh dear, what now?* I was beat. Just exhausted. *I'm in great pain, and I have nowhere to sleep.* Before she closed the door on me, she stated there were two hotels, actual hotels, close to the water, and I might have some luck there. I hung my head low as I apologized for my behavior and thanked her for the suggestions. I was running out of energy but knew I had to keep walking. I finally found the first hotel. Unfortunately, I would have to climb about ten steps, but it looked like fifty, just to make it to the door. *Oh my dear God, please help me.* I made it, slowly, to the door and into the entrance. It was a beautiful hotel with a grand entrance. I kissed my sticks for helping me make it to the top, and I prayed that they had rooms. *Oh please, dear Lord, let them have rooms.*

"What? You only have one left? I'll take it!" I said. I didn't care how much it cost at this point, even if this place was a five-star hotel. After she informed me of the price, my mouth dropped! It was twenty euros cheaper than La Casona! Wow, everything happens for a reason!

I paid my dues and crawled up to my spacious and impeccable room. I kissed my crutches, as I knew I would have never concluded the day without their assistance. I kissed my cross and said, "Thank you, Lord Jesus Christ, for helping me make it this far." The balcony view from my room was surreal. The hot shower erased the enormous amount of stress my body had endured. Standing there allowing this warm, relieving water to flow down every inch of body was absolute heaven. Regardless of the relief overall, my feet still did ache and reminded me that they needed more attention. I rubbed the swollen ankles gently with lotion and asked my dear Jesus to help me make it just a little bit longer for today.

I was starving and badly needed to refuel my beaten body with nourishment. I got dressed and limped my way to the nearest restaurant/bar I could find. I devoured another great authentic Spanish Menu del Dia and of couple of my favorite beverages. I mustered up enough strength to make it back to my room, and after my nightly routine and kisses, I crashed like I've never crashed before in my life! Boom!

CHAPTER 22

Day 10: August 31st, Adrin to →→Colunga - 8.7 Miles

Because you have made the LORD, who is my refuge,
Even the Most High, your dwelling place, No evil shall
befall you, nor shall any plague come near your dwelling;
For He shall give His angels charge over you, To keep you
in all your ways. In their hands they shall bear you up,
Lest you dash your foot against a stone.

—Psalm 91:9–12

After great contemplation, I decided to skip stages 16 and 17 because
I was getting way too far behind on my schedule. Even so, I had to
walk six miles from Adrin to Llanes just to get to a bus station that
would at least get me to Colunga. By the end of the day, I had walked
approximately 8.7 more miles on my poor feet.

The bus station in Llanes was easy to find, and it pleased me
greatly that it was only two or three euros. *Thank you, Lord, for helping
me get here.* The bus ride offered me temporary relief. I was getting

uncomfortable, as I wasn't sure where I was supposed to jump off the bus. I was sitting in the front seat, so I asked the knowledgeable driver if he could help me out. I informed him of the albergue I was looking for, and another gentleman sitting across from me entered our conversation and reassured me they would help me out. *Lord, you are so good to me.*

My exit was right in front of a beautiful and most magical church. *Thank you, Lord, for your purposeful blessings.* I thanked both of the men, and after I stepped out, the bus drove away.

I just stood there and admired this church before I turned and walked across the street to find the nearest bar. It was right there waiting for me. I purchased a beer and asked the bartender where I could find Confiteria las Palmas. He directed me across the street. Wow, so close—how awesome. After I finished a quick pincho and beer, I walked across the street to the other bar. I ordered another beer and a room. When she stated twenty-eight euros, I freaked out! I opened my guidebook and showed her that it's supposed to only be fifteen euros for pilgrims.

She replied, "It's August," in Spanish. Pretty much telling me it was peak season, so to pony up.

"Oh, okay." I had no vigor in me to argue, so I forked over my funds.

She summoned a young lady to escort me to my room. This was awkward. What was even more strange was the bartender who legally stole my money instructed me that this escort could not speak English or Spanish, and therefore I was not allowed to ask her any questions. I shrugged my shoulders and gave my nonverbal consent. I think this was a kind way of telling me this poor girl was mute. Anyway, this young girl escorted me back across the street, right next to the first bar I had visited.

There was an entrance, a simple door I would have never figured to be the entrance to the albergue. She took me up the stairwell, which was three infinite flights of stairs and treacherous for my feet, but I made it with the aid of my crutches. This place smelled old and looked old. The squeaky stairs, the peeling paint, and the cobwebs were far less than what you would expect from a one-star hotel. She showed me into a common area that reminded me of the Bates Hotel in the movie *Psycho*. If they had a scene in the lobby of the Bates Hotel, this is exactly what I would have expected. I followed her down a short hallway, where she showed me the common bathroom. Back down the hall to the common area, we walked across the living quarters to a door that she unlocked and showed me into. I was stunned what twenty-eight euros had bought me. It was tiny. A twin bed snug up to the corner, a tiny chest of drawers next to it, and a picture hanging crooked on the wall. That was it. I thanked her in hopes she couldn't read the dreadful disappointment on my face. With a painted smile, I said goodbye, and she disappeared without a word. Oh yeah, she can't speak.

Wow, just wow. I removed my backpack and plopped down on the bed from exhaustion and pain. Just as I did, all my disappointment was immediately erased by the view from my window. I could see the entire church. I almost couldn't breathe. How spectacular. God's holy house of worship was like a painting looking straight at me. It simply made me smile. After I admired it and had a short conversation with my Savior, I got up to look out the window.

It was a small, three-paned window angled in a way to create a small balcony. I dared not take my chances to stand on it though, as the windows were cracked and the spider webs were hanging sparingly. I could even see the sidewalk from small cracks on the flooring. It was okay, it would all be okay, knowing that my Lord would be watching over me.

I rested a short while before I got up, popped a few pills, and decided that I had to find a Laundromat close by. I had only one set of clean clothes left. I limped back down the stairs and down a few blocks. Even after asking several townspeople, no one could help me. My attempt to clean my clothes was unsuccessful. I accidentally ventured into a neighborhood where there were not any stores whatsoever before I realized I had walked too far. A silly thought crossed my mind. Maybe one of these houses would lend me their washer. That was farfetched. My feet couldn't tolerate any more for the day, so I had to retreat to my spider's cave, complete my nightly routine, and retire for the night. *I love you, Jay. I miss you. Please, God, watch over him and my family.*

CHAPTER 23

Day 11: September 1st, Colunga to Villaviciosa - 15.96 Miles

He who walks with wise men will be wise, But the companion of fools will be destroyed. Evil pursues sinners, But to the righteous, good shall be repaid.

—Proverbs 13:20–21

It took me a good seven hours to walk almost sixteen miles. My feet by the end of the day were punishing me severely. I prayed so much more today than yesterday, and I have found that I have been praying more and more each day. When you're walking alone, it's only you and God. We talk a lot. My faith in him has grown astronomically. I always thought that I was spiritual, but this walk is teaching me differently. I ask a lot of questions, and he's aware that I don't understand so many things. I don't understand why my feet are giving me such a hard time. Jay and I try to diagnose my feet issues every night, thinking it's got to be plantar fasciitis or heel spurs. Maybe pulled ligaments or inflamed tendons. Heaven only knows.

It's amazing that at all the albergues, I have seen numerous blisters on numerous pilgrims. People share all kinds of creams and lotions. I haven't gotten a single blister, thank goodness, but my feet are always swollen and painful. Why? I don't understand. Regardless, I keep thanking God for allowing me to walk one more day, one more mile. I thank him for making it tolerable enough for me to be able to take the next step. I laugh at myself because my twenty-five-year-old mind just wants to go, go, go, and my fifty-five-year-old body is refusing to keep up. They're just not on the same page. I started walking today so early that it was still dark outside. I don't know why I'm not scared in the dark, alone, in a foreign country, but I'm not. For some strange reason, I truly feel safe. I have this sense that he is watching over me.

As I passed Priesca, I had the honor of admiring one of the oldest churches on the Camino, the pre-Romanesque Church of San Salvador, which was built in AD 921. So mystical, so magical. It made me wonder how the entire world agrees and lives on the same linear time clock based on the life of one man. Jesus Christ, 921 AD. Wow.

I passed Sebrayo, followed by Tornón, and ultimately wandered into Villaviciosa, which means Vicious City. As I entered the outskirts of the city, I ran into Dave and his guitar along with two other pilgrims he had made friends with. Both of these young ladies were from Poland. Marta is a judge, and I found it encouraging that she was so young and already a judge. Her friend Kasia, who also worked in the judicial system, was also quite young. She tried to explain her position, but I couldn't quite grasp her duties or role.

It was well into the four o'clock hour when we found the albergue, but they only had two beds left. I really wasn't concerned because I had already booked a room at Casa España for only thirty-eight euros, which was not too far from the albergue. Dave stayed at a hotel across the street from mine. We decided to meet for dinner after everyone had an opportunity to unload and wash up. We would meet at six at an outdoor café.

As agreed upon, we all met at this nearby café and ordered drinks. People in Spain don't normally eat until after seven or eight. We were simply killing time with our stories and curious questions about each other's countries.

Out of nowhere, another pilgrim approached our table. He was an older Japanese man who introduced himself and asked if he could join us. Joyfully we all said yes, and he did so. All pilgrims are welcomed on the Camino! His name was Kenny, and he was a retired doctor. I believe he was in his mid-seventies and in great physical condition. After visiting with our new friend, we decided on which restaurant we would go experience. It was so enjoyable as we all sat at the table checking out each other's meals. "What did you get? Wow, that looks good." Food has the ability to bring so many people around the world together. It was so enjoyable, but suddenly I looked at my phone, and it was 9:45 p.m.

Oh heavens! I jumped up out of my chair and informed everyone that I had to run to the albergue that the girls had checked into because I had left my clothes to be laundered there, and they closed at 10:00 p.m. I apologized for having to leave, paid my tab, and tried to walk as fast as I could, which did not help my feet. Man, were my feet ever angry with me! I prayed hard for God to help me and to forgive me for losing focus. With much prayer and my sticks, I made it two minutes before they locked the doors. Amen! I could slither into clean clothes once again.

I made it back to my hotel. I enjoyed a milky-type liquor, which I bought at a small liquor store on my way back to the hotel. I poured it over ice, and it looked so scrumptious that I had to take a picture before I sipped on it slowly. Well, not too slowly, because it was so delicious, and it disappeared before I knew it. It did help me slip into a most pleasant slumber after my routine.

I thought about the day and how lucky I truly am. I think everyone in this fabulous world of ours should have these unbelievable experiences I am encountering on a daily basis. Thank you, Lord. I love you so very dearly.

CHAPTER 24

Day 12: September 2nd, Villaviciosa to Gijón - 17.7 Miles

But let him ask in faith, with no doubting, for he who doubts is like a wave of the sea driven and tossed by the wind.

—James 1:6

Just when I thought I had experienced the most miraculous miracle of my life, from not being able to stand to actually walking, today proved me wrong. God is so good; so beyond good is our God. Words cannot explain how much love I have for him and his presence in my life. Today was a day of pure and solid faith.

I got up early and was planning on a good start, but just as I closed the room door, I realized I had left my walking sticks right by the door inside and forgot to grab them. Oh heaven forbid. I knew for a fact that I could not make it on the journey without these miraculous crutches. I went down the stairs slowly, and even though no one was at the front desk, I saw a light on and heard some noise

133

coming from the kitchen. I went behind the counter and through the door and knocked on the wall, saying, "Hola, aye algen?" (Hello, is someone there?) I kept it up until finally someone appeared and asked if they could help me. I profusely apologized for bothering them but explained that I had left my sticks in the room and was wondering if they could open the door for me.

"Sí, sí, no problema." (Yes, yes, no problem).

I signed with relief. Thank you, Lord. They retrieved them for me, and I thanked them from the bottom of my heart.

It was still dark, yet even in the dark, this city was still so beautiful. Although I ended up walking over nine hours today, my feet never really carried me to Gijón. After a couple of hours of walking, I ran into Marta and Kasia, my new friends from Poland. It started raining, and Marta's raincoat was torn to shreds. It was not serving a purpose at all, so I told her to take mine. She kept refusing, stating I needed it, but I told her I had an extra one. I removed the one that Henry and Andrea had given me and gave it to her. She quickly put it on while I retrieved my backup one, which was a Mickey Mouse rain jacket that I had purchased at Walt Disney World, one of my most favorite places in the world.

The three of us walked together all the way to Peón, where we expected to eat at Casa Pepito. It didn't look open yet. It was 11:00 a.m., so for sure I thought it would have been open by now. It didn't take long to figure out they were closed on Wednesdays. Great, only on Wednesdays. Naturally, I live by Murphy's Law; therefore, it was Wednesday. They did leave access to a large seating area for pilgrims passing by, with numerous tables and chairs and several vending machines. Lunch now consisted of a hot Diet Coke, Furios, and Cheetos. Least bit appetizing, but at least it was something.

Conversing over our elaborate gourmet baggie lunch, Marta wanted to hear more about my friends who had given me the rain poncho. I went into my history with Henry and Andrea from Farmington. I told them about how fortunate I was to reside with them a few months during my young lost years of my early twenties.

They took me in like their child. I absolutely fell in love with their five-year-old daughter, Christine. She adopted me like I was her older sister. Christine and I had such a special relationship, which she was far too young to remember, but I would never forget. I promised her that one day I would name my daughter after her. I told Marta and Kasia I fulfilled that promise with my middle child, Gina Christine. They thought that was pretty cool.

We were having such a good time relaxing and talking, but I knew I needed to get started again because I had slowed down quite a bit and needed to make it to Gijón. I finished up my story and left my friends, as I knew it wouldn't take long for them to catch up to me. So I got up and left with a smile on my face.

Problem is these sweethearts never did catch up to me because somehow I got disoriented and lost. Being completely lost calls for constant prayer to help me find the next arrow or the next shell and so on and so forth. I did. I kept seeing them, but I wasn't sure it was the right direction because it didn't coincide with my guidebook.

I found myself on a paved road going up a mountain, with occasional traffic passing me in both directions. At one point, I decided to wave one down and stop a car to ask the driver if I was going in the right direction to Gijón. My feet were aching, painful, throbbing, and swollen, with a level of about a nine out of ten. It was a small car that slowed down, rolled down their window, and informed me that yes, the road did lead to Gijón. I felt a small degree of relief as I continued to struggle up this mountain road. I kept praying to my Lord for the next step and the next arrow.

After about another kilometer or two, I saw an arrow painted on a rock that pointed down the slope. I assessed the muddy, treacherous path and determined that it would certainly take me to the same road I was on. I concluded that I was just zigzagging on this switchback road that mountains normally have, so I would take this challenging, wet, somewhat dangerous trail downhill. I was certain it would get me closer to the town of Gijón. It was still drizzling, but my rain poncho was keeping me fairly dry, except of course my legs, socks, and hiking boots, which were drenched. I had already traveled down this path for about forty yards when I realized how truly dangerous it was becoming, but I just could not turn around now and go back up. I was already exhausted, and my feet were terribly painful, literally screaming. I was hungry and just ready to drop, but I kept praying to my Lord Jesus for the next step. *Please God, help me. I can't do this without you.* The trail was getting more and more dangerous as small streams of water were trickling on both sides of me. It was so muddy, and every step had to be very calculated to assure I would not slip and roll down the remainder of the slope. *Oh my God, I need you.* It was getting worse the further down I went. I was hurting so badly, and I was getting more and more scared of falling. My crutches prevented so many opportunities for me just lose it all and roll down into a severe injury. I prayed and prayed and prayed harder for every step I was taking. It just would not end. Thank goodness the sticks had steel points, as they would dig deep into the wet mud and find security in order for me to take another step. Two or three dozen more times, these wonderful heaven-sent crutches prevented me from slipping down this scary, relentless trail.

I was running out of energy, my body was weakening with every step, and my constant praying became the air I was inhaling. *Please, dear Lord, oh please help me. Please, God, keep me safe. Please help me take another step. Oh dear God, I'm in so much pain, please help me.* My exhaustion was getting the best of me. The downward, fierce, and unforgiving trail was mutilating me, punching me in the ribs, knocking the breath out of my gasping lungs. The wind was slapping my face like an upset mother, and the rain began to pound every inch of my exposed skin. The beating I was taking was like the devil trying to thin out my faith, but I dared not even give a thought in that direction. I kept my God, my hope, and my strong, powerful faith in him as my final fuel to take the next step until at last I reached the very bottom of this horrific path.

It should have been a great relief, but as I stood there thinking I had conquered it, I glanced and saw a rock with a yellow arrow pointing upward. My jaw dropped. I couldn't even comprehend what I was looking at. I was in disbelief. There was absolutely no possible way. Not even an ounce of will was left in my body, my mind, my heart, or my spirit. I was broken. I began to tear up. *Oh dear God, please, I can't do it anymore. Please help me. Please, dear Lord, please send me an angel. I need an angel so desperately.* I started to cry because I simply did not know what to do.

I had to figure something out, as I knew I had reached the very bottom of my energy and practically of my existence. My beaten body couldn't take another beating. My feet felt like they were going to fall off. I felt like the alcoholic that had finally reached the very bottom of his drinking problem and could only look to God for answers and hope for recovery. As I turned around, about thirty yards from me was a small cinderblock house with a small black car parked in front of it. A thin man had just walked out the front door, and immediately, without thought, I started yelling at him.

"Señor, señor!" I waved my arm for him to come in my direction. Luckily for me, he did. The rain by now had gone back to a constant drizzle, so I knew he was getting wet on my account. When he was close enough, I asked him, "¿El Camino está subiendo?" (The Camino is up?) as I pointed up the hill.

He responded, "Sí," as he nodded his head yes.

Oh heaven forbid. I began begging him. I told him I couldn't take another step and offered to pay him good money if he could give me a ride to Gijon.

He apologized and said, "No es mi auto. Pero ven, avenir conmigo, ven a conocer mi familia, ven." (It's not my car, but come, come with me. Come and meet my family, come.)

He was walking back toward this house as he was motioning for me to follow him. At this point, I gave my entire self to God. I was his. I belong to him and him alone. I can't explain the feeling when you have absolutely nothing left but your faith in Jesus Christ, and therefore, whatever was to happen was completely in his hands. I gave my total soul to my Lord, for I had no idea what this man was leading me into. I prayed to God with the very last ounce of spiritual energy I had to please take care of me. I prayed that I wasn't making a mistake. *Please, Lord, be with me.*

Luke 22:42 says, "Father, if it is your will, take this cup from Me; nevertheless not My will, but Yours, be done."

I had no idea what was awaiting me inside that door.

"Por favor, ven y conocer a mi familia, déjame ayudarte con tu impermeable." (Please, please come in and meet my family. Let me help you with your raincoat.)

He was motioning for me to come inside with his hand as he was introducing himself, "Mi nombre es Jose." (My name is Joe).

I walked through the small doorway, and he started to assist me in removing my drenched raincoat.

"Deja que te ayude," (Let me help you) he said in the process. In this tiny little cottage I had just stepped into was the kitchen with a table where there sat a lovely lady, approximately my age if not younger, and he introduced her as his sister-in-law. Her name was Barbara, and she was the lady of the house. Hovering over the small antique-looking stove was her husband, Jose's brother. His name was Paco. Another gentleman was sitting at the table. Jose introduced him as Christian, and he was the next-door neighbor.

"Hola, mi nombre es Marissa, y soy un peregrina de Texas." (Hello, my name is Marissa, and I am a pilgrim from Texas.)

Wow, you wouldn't believe how all their eyes just widened. *Wow, we have a real Texan in our house!* That was basically the response I received as soon as I finished my sentence. For some strange reason, they found that fact to be beyond incredible.

Immediately, Barbara motioned me over and invited me to sit next to her, pulling back the chair next to her. As soon as I sat down, she offered me a glass of champagne! I graciously accepted and experienced immediate relief to my feet as soon as the pressure subsided. *Oh thank you, Lord.* Barbara was pouring me a glass of champagne while Paco, her husband, started to serve dinner. She asked if I would please stay for dinner and visit for a short while, get a little rest, and then Jose would give me a ride to Gijón, as he had informed her of my needs while he was helping me with my raincoat. I told them I didn't want to be a burden, and they all insisted it was not a bother at all but rather of great pleasure to host a pilgrim, especially one from Texas.

Jose had taken my drenched rain poncho out back to shake off the excess water and hung it out to dry. We had begun a very friendly, engaging conversation, so I was at ease immediately. I was astonished that not even five minutes ago, I had reached the very bottom of my hope, begging God to save me, and now I was sitting at the most welcoming, inviting, and loving table with the friendliest, kindest people in the world, getting ready to eat the most authentic Spanish meal I would ever get to experience on this pilgrimage. And to top it off, I was drinking a glass of extraordinary champagne! This incredible moment made me wonder how some people cannot believe that God exists.

The next two hours were the deepest, most inspiring and meaningful experiences of my entire pilgrimage. This is the true and powerful meaning of God's existence. Man is authentically good in nature, and taking care of each other, offering friendship and kindness, especially to strangers, spreads endless love around the world. It makes the world a better place in every aspect. God is good, and doing good is the Godly way. These were the angels I had begged him for just moments ago. Even though I only asked him for one, he sent me four. I had instantly been saved, and my faith multiplied infinitely.

As Paco was serving the appetizer, he explained they were fresh tomatoes picked earlier that morning from their garden. He had glazed them in olive oil and a special seasoning. He stated that he and Christian took turns cooking dinner. Tonight it was his turn, and tomorrow night they would eat at Christian's house next door, also made of cinderblocks with a few *cabritos* (goats) and chickens roaming around. I found myself in the authentic deep woods of Spain. Christian stated they took turns because they were both retired, and Barbara was the only one who worked, at a nearby hospital. With what I was trying to understand, it sounded like she did phlebotomy for the hospital and a home health agency. She was also going to school to finish her nursing degree, so when I told her I was a nurse, it was like, *Wow!* We really connected. I told her I had been a nurse for about twenty-eight years. I couldn't encourage her enough to finish her education, as it was the most rewarding career one could ever ask for. Helping people feel better is my passion, my calling, but at this moment, I was the one being cared for, and I graciously accepted it. Barbara and I continued our nursing conversations, and intermittently, Paco would explain his fabulous dishes he was serving. You could tell he was very proud of his cooking skills, and I couldn't wait to be the recipient of them.

Our next course was a bean soup followed by the main dish, which was a vegetable and chicken mixture that was absolutely scrumptious. No need to mention that it all came from the backyard. Also served were chorizo links and tripe. Everything was so delicious I was devouring it. Paco continued elaborating on his cooking skills. It was funny and enjoyable.

They asked me numerous questions about Texas. I had to disappoint them and informed them that most of us don't ride horses but that we still like to wear cowboy hats and boots. They bragged about how much they knew about John Wayne and all his movies. We laughed so much. I just couldn't help falling in love with this family.

Christian too had to put his two cents in regarding his skills. He was a retired jewelry maker and even ran home to retrieve a small cigar box filled with a few of his prized pieces. It was full of rings and necklace pieces he had designed. His pride and joy was a piece he made from a coin that he cut, drilled, and shaped into this incredible necklace. I was so impressed because it was so unique. I offered to buy it from him, but he just couldn't part with it no matter how much I offered. It was priceless. I remember when I crawled into bed that night, I tried to draw it in my journal so that maybe someday I would have it remade and inscribe his name behind it, "Designed by Christian."

Two hours passed by in what seemed like two minutes. After dinner, they enjoyed their coffee and cigarettes, and I just continued enjoying their company. It was just after seven when Barbara told Jose to fetch the keys and to get me to Gijón so that I could get some rest. She was so incredibly kind, and I just couldn't thank God enough for bringing them into my path. Everything happens for a reason. While I was getting up, Jose went to retrieve my poncho that had pretty much dried off. Barbara told me to wait momentarily, as she had something to give me. She went into a tiny room next to the kitchen and returned with something in her closed hand.

She grabbed my hands and said, "Así que siempre te accordarás de nosotros, por favor ponte esto para trabajar para mí." (So that you will always remember us, please wear this to work for me.) I opened my hand, and in it was placed a small nurse angel.

My mouth dropped open. "Oh my dear heavenly Jesus! You are so good to me." I remembered again that I had asked him for an angel, and although I couldn't take these four home with me, I was taking their memory with me in this angel pin she had presented me with. I was astounded. I looked into her heavenly eyes and promised her I would wear it to work every single day. To this day, I have fulfilled that promise, for I have made it a permanent part of my name badge. I hugged and said goodbye to everyone and knew in my heart that God had gifted me with an extraordinary experience. I didn't want to leave, but I knew I had to in order to continue my journey.

Angel pin gift from Barbara

Jose helped me as I limped to the car. He loaded up my backpack and rain poncho in the back seat. We continued with our friendly conversation as we drove for approximately fifteen to twenty minutes before we finally arrived at Gijón. That was several more miles I would have never survived. Thank you, Lord, for taking care of me.

Jose did have a little difficulty locating the hotel where I had made a reservation. He went as far as parking illegally in the middle of surrounding traffic. We walked about half a block from the car to where he thought it might be. I was barely able to take each step, and my ankles and feet felt like they belonged to someone else much larger than I. He felt so bad watching me walk with great difficulty, especially when he found out we were at the wrong place. He was so apologetic for making me walk unnecessarily. I tried my hardest to let him know I was okay and that none of this was his fault. I still struggled to get back to the car.

He had asked for the appropriate directions, so now he was assured of getting me to the right place. It was around the corner across from the canal of water, which was not far at all. He also showed me where the bus station was so that I wouldn't have a hard time finding it in the morning, in case I decided to utilize it.

What was going to seem like an eternity was the walk from the car to the front desk of the correct hotel. Jose grabbed my things and helped me load up. He pointed me to the front door of the hotel, and I'll never forget what he said.

"Tengo una gran pena." (I have great pity.) He was almost in tears, wanting to carry me to the door, but I promised him I was going to be just fine, and I greatly appreciated his sincerity. I felt so bad that I was making him feel so bad.

Before I said goodbye, I grabbed his hand and placed a folded-up fifty-euro bill in his hand and instructed him to please tell Paco, Barbara, Christian, and himself to have an elaborate meal on me. I would never ever forget their kindness and generosity. We hugged and gestured goodbye the correct España way, a kiss on each cheek.

I began my short but lengthy, crippled crawl to the hotel as he drove away. After checking in and managing to make it up a flight of stairs to my room, I collapsed on the bed. I popped my pills and decided to call my podiatrist, Dr. Aeby's office, just to let him know what I was going through and to get some recommendations. It was 8:00 p.m. my time in Spain, but that meant it was 9:00 a.m. in Corpus Christi. I spoke to his secretary, as he was already seeing patients, but she said she would deliver my message. I explained my symptoms and what I had tried so far and said that I was taking tons of ibuprofen but only every six hours, not every four. The instructions returned rapidly from my doc. It certainly sounded like plantar fasciitis. I was told to continue the ibuprofen, buy some shoe supports to slip into my boots, exercise my feet, and to put my boots on while I was still in bed before I got up for the day. Most importantly, he sent a message for me to take a day off! *What? Oh man.*

What was coincidental is that my guidebook stated that my next day's walk "is the least enjoyable stage of walking on the Camino del Norte." The wonderful family I was honored to have dinner with also informed me how ugly my walk would be tomorrow, mostly because it was all paved roads and I would be passing nothing but industrial settings. They all encouraged me to skip it. It was simple arithmetic. I added these three sources together and concluded to comply with all recommendations and take the bus to Aviles.

I called Jay and had an extremely long conversation with him. I told him about my extraordinary experience with this family and how much they had helped me. I told him about my phone call to my podiatrist, and he immediately wanted to take credit for diagnosing my problem before my podiatrist did. Jay had this problem before and was certain I was going through the same thing. I prayed, I Facebooked my sister and friends, I prayed again, I smiled at God, and I prayed myself to sleep.

CHAPTER 25

Day 13: September 3rd, Gijón to Aviles - 3 Miles

Ask, and it will be given to you; seek, and you will find; knock, and it will be opened to you.

—Matthew 7:7

The moment I woke up, I remembered what my podiatrist had instructed me to do. *Put your boots on before you get out of bed.* I got dressed while still lying down. A little awkward, but I'd do anything that would help my feet.

The bus station was only two blocks away from the hotel. So far, so good. I was quite a bit early and was the second person in line to board bus number 2. Coincidently, it took twenty minutes to go twenty-two kilometers.

I remember looking out the window and seeing all the industrial parks Barbara and Paco had told me about. The numerous tall stacks with black smoke willowing out like snakes dancing into the clouds. It was definitely reassurance that I had made the right decision.

As soon as I stepped off the bus and readjusted all my belongings, I immediately began asking people where the nearest tourist office was so that I could retrieve a map of Aviles and figure out where to go. I needed to find the albergue, and my guidebook was not helpful, as there were certainly no directions from the bus station. What was really amusing was that every person I stopped to ask gave me different directions. One old man and his wife actually started arguing about it. I felt so bad that I had started a domestic quarrel. I finally found an office that not only provided me with a map but even drew a line straight to the albergue.

I was fortunate enough to run into a gorgeous church, where I took some pictures, said a prayer, and lit a candle. It was breathtaking. I walked slowly, utilizing my crutches up and down all the stairs, and by the grace of God, I never stumbled. My feet were tolerating a level of about five or six out of ten, as the ibuprofen had kicked in, so I was able to walk to the albergue without great difficulty.

I stopped at a café and ordered half a sandwich and espresso with Baileys. Why is it that Baileys makes such a superb creamer? I could get used to that. I walked through a nice park and took lots of pictures. I also took pictures of the beautiful buildings Aviles has to brag about. I stopped at another bar and had a beer just to kill more time because the albergue didn't open until 1:00 p.m. I arrived at the albergue at 12:35 p.m. and was of course the first one in line.

The hospitalero spoke excellent English, so when I asked him where he was from, he replied, "Chicago."

"Wow! So what are you doing here?" I asked.

He and his wife had been living there for the past three years. He taught English as a second language for a company that wanted all their employees to learn English. He was a banker and an accountant back in the States. He held no teaching degree whatsoever. Problem was he couldn't find a job in his field, and this teaching opportunity fell into his lap, which was very fortunate for him. I asked him how he could be teaching without a degree, and he stated the company he worked for didn't want formal English to be taught but rather just conversational English. This made it easy for him, as this he was capable of doing. He had been doing it for the past three years and volunteered his extra time to the albergue because he loved visiting and meeting pilgrims from all over the world. He and his wife loved Spain, and I could certainly understand why. I, as well, had fallen in love with Spain.

When I located a bunk on the lower level, I made sure it was as close to the bathroom as possible for a "just in case" morning. The unfortunate thing was I didn't have an electric outlet anywhere close to my bunk, so I asked another pilgrim if I could borrow the one close to his bunk. One thing I found on the pilgrimage was that all pilgrims were so accommodating to each other. It was one big, happy, worldwide family. Everyone looked out for one another even as complete strangers. Kindness was ample.

I ran into Kenny again, the Japanese gentleman I had met in Villaviciosa. He noticed my severely impaired gait. His kindness perfused out of his skin. He handed me six patches that looked like lidocaine patches, except that they were tan in color, and the only writing I could understand was 100 mg. I remembered Kenny is a retired doctor, and he said they were for pain relief. He applied one on each of my heels and told me to sleep with my socks on so that they would stay in place. I was so thankful and told him I didn't know how to repay him. He expressed how it made him feel good being able to help—naturally, a medical professional's personality trait.

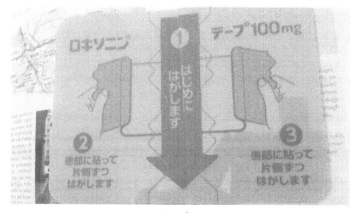

Patches

I planted myself into my bunk after a very early dinner, which was spent outside in the albergue patio where several pilgrims were sharing their food and stories. I had lots of conversations with familiar pilgrims and some new ones too. I listened to my music, Facebooked, and prayed. *Thank you, Lord, for a day of mostly rest. Thank you, Kenny, for the patches. Thank you, sister Thelma and all my Facebook friends, for all the prayers you have been sending.* I telephone kissed my special sweetheart, Jay, good night and fell asleep with a smile.

CHAPTER 26

Day 14: September 4th, Aviles to Muros de Nalón - 20.2 Miles

"Therefore I say to you, whatever things you ask for when you pray, believe that you receive them, and you will have them."

—Mark 11:24

A pilgrim's quiet movement woke me this morning. I had not set my alarm because I had left my phone charging next to the sweet pilgrim by the window. I had no idea what time it was, as the vast majority of the albergue was still in peaceful darkness. Some final snores were still taking place. I packed up my things quietly and grabbed my phone on the way out. I looked at my phone; it displayed 6:40 a.m. *Awesome. I love early starts.*

It was still very dark when I departed, but I had mapped out my route up to Avienda Armania and found my way. I amused myself as I continued kissing my two left fingers and raising them up to the sky while delivering a loving thank you to my Lord. Every time I saw my next arrow or shell, there went my auto-kisses. At times I find myself asking him loudly, "Okay, God, where's my next sign?" Within seconds, there it was. I really thought I would do well today with my feet, but after about nine or ten miles, which took me almost five hours, they really started hurting. I had replaced the patches Kenny had given me. It also started raining, and I struggled just trying to put my Mickey Mouse rain poncho on, but I managed. I had purchased a package of wafers the day before, and I fought with my poncho, struggling to get them out of my backpack without removing the thing. After struggling for about ten minutes, I finally managed to acquire these silly wafers. I laughed at myself for accomplishing such a feat.

While trying to enjoy these delicious cookies, the pain in my feet took over the vast majority of my thought process, and I found myself starting to get very depressed. I was getting really down because I couldn't understand why I had to struggle so much to take every step. After the fifth hour, they just kept getting worse and worse, even after gulping down my ibuprofen. I got to the point where I just had a major meltdown, and I just cried and cried and cried. Yes, to some degree of the pain but mostly because I couldn't understand why simple walking was so difficult. I couldn't understand what was wrong with me. I begged God to carry me and help me make it to my next destination. I truly thought for a while that I wasn't going to make it, but I simply focused on my faith and asking God to be with me, begging him to help me put one foot in front of the other. I felt confident, as my rescue crutches kept reminding me that I wasn't alone. There came the next step, the next arrow, the next sign with the next prayer.

Besides being exhausted and in pain, I had the sudden urge to go to the bathroom, both number one and number two. I kept thinking about crawling into the deep woods surrounding me and taking care of business, but I just couldn't bring myself to do it. Certainly I would be busted. So I continued pushing myself through the pain and fighting the urge. I told myself along the way that it just didn't make sense that I was pushing myself beyond my body's limit. Somehow I was going to have to figure out a way to continue walking but still take care of my feet. I finally concluded that I could only handle about ten or so miles a day before they started burning. Therefore, tomorrow, I would check to see if I could take a bus, taxi, or train halfway to my next stop and walk the rest of the way. Brilliant. I could continue my walk to the best of my ability and not burn my feet off by day's end.

> For it is written: "He will command his angels charge over you, To keep you."
> —Luke 4:10

When I saw the sign to the hostel Casa Carmen, I was ever so thankful and relieved. I kissed my canes and my cross, thanked the Lord, and limped my way up to the receptionist desk, only to be greeted by an absolutely beautiful, drop-dead gorgeous angel. God named this one Sarah. Another true blessing had entered my confused and painful world. Sarah not only drew me a map to the train station but even said that if time allowed after breakfast, she would give me a ride there personally.

Two other pilgrims had walked in, so Sarah gave the three of us the entire spill about staying at La Casa Carmen. Dinner was served from 7:00 to 8:00 p.m. for ten euros, and we had to place our order now! I placed mine immediately, as I wasn't about to walk anywhere else for the day. Checkout was by 9:00 a.m. Breakfast would be served between 7:30 and 8:30 a.m., and that cost would be three euros. It would cost sixteen euros to stay the night, and Tony, the host, would show us to our bunks and bathroom.

After I removed my backpack and unloaded, I walked back up to the front desk to order a beer. Sarah informed me I could sit outside, and she would bring it to me. To my surprise, Sarah served me a beer, brought me pinchos on the house, and then returned with a large bowl of ice water in which to soak my feet. I was again amazed at the graciousness of my Lord for bringing another heaven-sent angel to me. She was so kind and thoughtful. I could almost see the wings on her back. Truly a breath of fresh air.

The ice water really helped numb my feet for a while. It felt so good. I paid a few euros for Tony to wash my clothes, but there was no dryer, so after they were finished washing, I would have to go hang them on a clothesline to dry. While they were washing, it dawned on me that I had left my cross necklace and some money in my short's pocket. I went crazy, thinking I had lost my cross. I kissed my beautiful diamond cross frequently, and it had sentimental value, so I asked Tony if he could kindly look for it. He did, and he found it in the washing machine! Bless his heart. He placed it safely back into my hands, along with my lost money. I told him I would be forever grateful in Spanish and then tipped him twenty euros for being successful. That seemed to make him happy, as he walked away smiling. I was just so incredibly thankful it had not been lost. I had budgeted for tipping funds, but several times now, some came up unexpected. This was one of them.

I enjoyed another fabulous dinner and crawled into bed by 8:00 p.m. I lay there feeling so very blessed and thankful.

"Thank you, God, for being so good to me. Thank you for getting me this far, and thank you for all the angels you are sending me." My faith just grows and grows on a daily basis.

CHAPTER 27

Day 15: September 5th, Muros de Nalón to Santa Maria - 9 Miles

---

But do not forget to do good and to share, for with such sacrifices God is well pleased.

—Hebrews 13:16

Someone else's alarm clock awakened my senses well before my own went off. My anxious self was ready to get another early start. I got dressed, repacked, and was ready for my three-euro breakfast, which consisted of toast, butter, marmalade, coffee cake, a banana (which I saved for a later snack), orange juice, and espresso coffee. Not bad for three euros.

Sarah, my sweet new angel, receptionist, bartender, maid, and probably owner of the place, graciously gave me that ride to the train station she had offered. This lovely lady wakes up beautiful. Truly she hadn't combed her hair, washed up, or even gotten changed and was stunningly gorgeous. *I want to wake up like that*, I thought to myself.

We had a nice conversation in a short period, as the station was not far. I found out she loves to collect foreign currency and rattled on how she had collected some from several different nations. She went above and beyond, not only giving me a ride, but she got out of her car in her pajamas and slippers and walked me into the station. There was no one in the room. These stations are all automated and coin operated. She helped me purchase my ticket, which was 1.80 euros, and then gave me instructions to stay in the station because it was still cold outside. She told me in fifteen minutes to go outside and stand on the platform where the train would see me and stop. She showed me where to insert the ticket, where the machine would spit it back out, and informed me the glass gates would open, allowing me to pass and go to the platform. *God, your blessings are endless. Thank you for this beautiful angel.*

I wanted to give her something for her troubles and generosity, but as I was trying to remove money from my fanny pack, she instantly stopped me and refused. To her, she said, this was all a simple act of kindness; paying her would change that, and therefore she would not accept a tip. She insisted I place it back in my fanny pack.

"Okay." I told her in Spanish to wait. I withdrew an American twenty-dollar bill and wrote a message: "You are an angel. Thank you so very much for everything you did for me. God be with you. Always, Marissa."

Now she couldn't turn it down, as it was nothing more than a thank-you card, I told her as I stuffed it in her pocket. She laughed. We hugged, and she departed. Thanks again, God.

The fifteen minutes passed by quickly, and I did as I was instructed by Sarah. I wasn't out on the platform for more than a minute or two before another couple came and joined me to wait for the train. They initiated a conversation with me, noting that I was a pilgrim with my backpack and shell hanging on it. They were so friendly. I wondered if this happens in New York while people are waiting for the subway.

I told them I was on the Camino but that my feet were giving me a very hard time and that I could not walk as far as I had planned on a daily basis. They were on their way to Ribadeo for vacation and reassured me they would help me with my train ride. The train was there in no time, and we jumped on board. The conductor was also very sweet and helpful and stated he would let me know ahead of time that my stop would be next. So kind. I thought about how God works, handing me from one angel to another and then another and so on and so forth.

> Fear not, for I am with you; Be not dismayed, for I am your God. I will strengthen you, Yes, I will help you, I will uphold you with My righteous right hand.
> —Isaiah 41:10

When I got off at my stop and the train departed, I suddenly felt abandoned. It was completely empty. Not a soul in sight. I didn't know exactly where I was or where to go. I pulled my guidebook out and tried to figure out my coordinates. I thought that maybe a road I saw was the one on the map in my book, so after a prayer, I went ahead and took it. Continued prayers kept me going in that direction. There was no one around to ask. At last I saw a highway, but just as I turned around, I saw a sign for the Camino. Oh, I was ever so relieved. I kissed my cross and thanked my Lord.

It was now 9:50 a.m., and I started walking up this unpredictable trail, the first of many unforgiving trails for today. I cried so many times. First, over my distorted and damaged feet for giving me so much trouble. Then I cried for my children, my life, my job, my mom. Just cried for every reason I could think of. After so many tears, I figured out I was crying tears of joy. I focused on all my blessing in my life. I realized how happy I was with my life. I was crying for my happy life. My boyfriend Jay, my home, my routine, and that I wouldn't change a thing. I also prayed that a few things would change that I had no control over, but with faith and prayer, perhaps in the future they would. I found myself getting very emotional on these trails. So challenging, these trails felt like a boxer's gloves punching at my feet while they served as the punching bag. Every step was just an intentional punch. But I would not give up, and with lots of prayer, I finally made it to Santa Maria.

I walked into the bar and told the bartender, an old man named Raul, that I had a reservation. He escorted me across the street to my room. He then informed me dinner was at seven and showed me how to use the key. I said farewell and that I would see him in a few. I plopped myself in the bed. *Oh my goodness, thank you, Jesus. Now to round up enough energy to shower, change, and get this ailing body back across the street to eat. I have no idea how I am managing other than my faith in God. I cannot think of another time in my life that my perseverance in faith has been so challenged.*

The shower felt so wonderful. I was so thankful I had a private room. I was certain I would have a good night's rest. I wobbled back to the bar and ordered my Menu del Dia and a beer. I sat alone in a large dining area, obviously not a very busy place. Perhaps because it was such a small town? The meal was fabulous, or maybe my hunger just made it seem that good.

The lady working the bar gave me a bag of ice to take to my room and use on my feet before I left. Apparently, she had noticed my limping and knew I was hurting. I thanked her for her sincerity and slowly, very painfully, made it back to the room.

That night was one of the most miserable ones I had yet to experience. I didn't use the ice for my heels because, for some bizarre reason, a tendon, muscle, or ligament on the inner aspect of my right knee was hurting so horribly. It became excruciatingly painful to the point it would not allow me to fall asleep. This pain was new and came from nowhere. I had not twisted, fallen, or sustained any kind of injury that I could fault for its sudden appearance, so I couldn't understand what I had done to make it hurt so very bad. The ice was having little to no impact. I thought I had cried enough today, but my tear ducts got another workout. *God, please help me. Please make this go away.* I was so miserable. I was beyond miserable. I was out of ibuprofen, and therefore, all I had left was prayer. I finally prayed myself to sleep.

CHAPTER 28

Day 16: September 6th, Santa Maria to Ribadeo - 4 Miles

A man's heart plans his way, But the Lord directs his steps.
—Proverbs 16:9

Apparently, I must have cried myself to sleep. My pillow was moist. I woke up with some vivid scenes of dreams I had, some very colorful and delightful scenes. One quite cheerful one was I was at a museum, standing and admiring a huge Disney print. It was not a painting; it was a print of the rabbit in *Alice in Wonderland* having tea with the Beast from *Beauty and the Beast*. I remember wanting to buy it, but unfortunately it was not for sale.

In another scene, my daughter Nikki was giving me a ride to my next destination. I of course am riding shotgun, just rattling on in a happy conversation. I thought to myself when I thought about that dream, *My daughter must be praying for me and loves me to death to get herself all the way over here to Spain just to give me a ride.* My silliness made me crack a smile. Regardless of these wonderful dreams, I still woke up in excruciating pain and had great difficulty making it to the bathroom. When I looked at myself in the mirror, I just finally broke down and said I was done. I could not go on mutilating my feet, as clearly there was something terribly wrong with them. I had to start taking care of them, so I came to terms with the fact that I would have to rearrange the rest of my schedule. I was done trying to impress myself. I now had to concentrate on how I was going to accomplish walking the last one hundred kilometers, which is approximately sixty miles, in order to earn my Compostela. I would review my schedule once I got on the train, which was in Ballota, a good four kilometers away. I came to terms that this was no longer my plan, and I had to allow God to take over.

I got an extremely early start, probably 6:00 a.m., giving me at least three hours to get to Ballota. I should have tried to find the train station in Santa Maria, which, come to find out, would have only been two kilometers, but I didn't figure that out until it was far too late. That morning was the first time I had to use my headlight, which I had been carrying in my backpack since I started. It was pitch black outside, the scary type of darkness you see in horror movies. This darkness was different from all the other mornings, but I couldn't place my finger on why.

I thought about how I got the headlight as I was placing it over my head and on to my forehead. It was a gift from a guy I met at Sharkathon the previous year. I remembered his name was Patrick. I thought about the scene on the beach at about ten o'clock at night, waiting in this long line trying to register for the tournament that would start on the following morning. Practically everyone was wearing one except me, so he handed me his, stating he had several and that I could keep it. It came in so very handy this morning, so I thanked him again as I was placing it on my forehead. There weren't even any streetlights flickering anywhere in sight. It was truly pitch black. The trails were awful and scary. They were muddy and dangerous, never mind the darkness.

Resorting to prayer, each step that I didn't slip and fall was my saving grace. Nonstop prayers kept me going regardless of the danger or the pain. Thank you, Patrick, for the headlight, or I wouldn't have been able to see where I was going to step next.

It was daybreak by the time I got off the muddy trail and onto a paved road. Now the next challenge was to find the train depot. I used my guidebook and maps on my phone and ventured off the Camino. I didn't see a soul for about the next two hours, until finally a little old lady was on her morning walk, and as she was passing me by, I asked her if I was going the right way to the train depot. When she told me I had passed it, I just hung my head in an "oh no" fashion, saying to myself, "Thanks a lot, Murphy." I wanted to burst out in tears, but I held my composure. *Don't cry, Marissa. Just stay calm and be cool.*

I couldn't figure out why there were no signs for a train stop. I was certain I had not seen any. She saw the great disappointment in my nonverbal gestures and started making friendly conversation as I turned around and started walking back where I had come from. She slowed down her pace a great deal because she clearly saw that something was wrong with my gait. I explained that there was something wrong with my feet, as they hurt quite a bit, but that I was still able to walk. We encountered another local, a gentleman, so she stopped him for reassurance that she was taking me in the right direction. He told her yes and that it was within a few yards from us. I couldn't believe it! I had passed it, but there was no way I would have ever known, not only because there were no signs but because it was just a dirt trail that led into a forest. She actually walked down the dirt trail with me and showed me where it was. Nicely hidden, surrounded by all the trees. Wow. Who in the world would have ever known unless you were a local?

It was one of those glass, open shelters, almost like the one in Comillas where I was waiting for the bus that never came. This one had two benches though. I asked her where I was supposed to buy the tickets, because I saw no machines. She told me not to worry about it, as the conductor would come by and collect once I got on board. I thanked her for her extreme kindness and apologized for interrupting her morning walk. Before she left, she told me I would have to wave the train down, as this was not a mandatory stop. I thanked her once more as this wonderful, sweet angel departed back up the dirt path.

Due to my early departure, I was forty-five minutes early. I needed the rest anyway and propped my poor, aching feet onto the bench and on my backpack for some elevation. The train arrived exactly at 9:30 a.m. I waved it down, and it stopped just as she said it would. I gladly jumped on board, and the moment I was inside, a broad smile crossed my face. I saw a familiar face. Lo and behold, it was the same friendly conductor from my previous ride. Best of all, he remembered me. After I paid him 6.80 euros for my ride, he told me to go to the very back of the train, where it was much more quiet and private. He said I could get better pictures from the window, so I complied. He was very friendly and talkative and made me feel at ease. He left me alone in the back of the train, and I indeed appreciated the beautiful countryside of Spain. I took numerous pictures and listened to my music. He came back around when he knew it was time for me to get off in Ribadeo. He gave me instructions on what street to walk down in search for a pharmacy, as I had told him I was out of my ibuprofen and needed a refill.

I did as my kind conductor instructed, but I always manage to get myself confused, so I had to start asking around for a pharmacy. I was easily given directions and stocked up with enough ibuprofen to get me home on. *My poor kidneys and gut lining. I hope they survive this abuse.* I took two immediately, thanked the employee, and went next door to order a burger and fries. I hadn't had American food in a while, so I was really going to enjoy this splurge. Needless to say, I did.

My next challenge was to find my hotel, Santa Cruz. I was able to navigate this big city utilizing my maps and following signs, but when I got there, they didn't have a single bed for me. Maybe that was a good thing because I really didn't feel very safe. It just appeared to be in a not-so-safe part of town. I came to that conclusion just by the way it was kept up. At least the sweet receptionist called another hotel to try to help me find a room. Lucky for me, he did. He said there was a Hotel RosMary not too far, and they would hold a room for me. On top of that, he said they would give me the same rate since he was referring me and I didn't have a reservation with them.

I had no trouble finding the hotel. What was really cool was that it was right next to another spectacular church. I went in to admire it and say a prayer.

My room was comfortable. I rested just a bit and then went to ask the clerk for directions to the bus station. She gave them to me, stating it was about half a mile away. My feet were under control, and I was sure I could make it. I needed to go see what their schedules looked like so I could get a better idea of how to plan my tomorrow.

I was so terribly confused looking at their schedules. If I was interpreting correctly, they had two runs, one at 6:30 a.m. and another at 2:45 p.m. I decided quickly that I would finally take a day and sleep in to rest my tired soles. While I was walking the streets to find the station, I realized how many bars this city had. I lost count after about three thousand. I chose one random one and went in to rest and enjoy some grandma juice. I spent a little time writing, listening to music, and finally relaxing. I found my way back to the hotel and gave my little feet a double take of rest. They enjoyed that immensely. I got up later in the evening, got dressed, and went to have a fabulous dinner. Upon returning to the room, I spoke to Jay. We hadn't spoken in a couple days, so I was really missing him. I thank my lucky stars for this man and am so very glad he is the one I am going home to. You know you're madly in love when you have numerous conversations with someone who's not even there. I love you, baby.

I was starting to get over my disappointment of not walking the entire 450 miles I had planned. I realized I was very lucky to even be there, and even though I was walking a lot less per day, the fact that I was even walking gave me immense joy. I was not going to cry for cutting my miles down; I would be thankful for the ones I did get to walk. *I don't know how I'm doing this walk with the condition my feet are in, but as long as God allows me to get up out of bed, stand, and place one foot in front of the other, by golly I'm going to just keep on doing that. Thank you, Lord Jesus. You are so good to me.*

CHAPTER 29

Day 17: September 7th, Ribadeo to Baamonde - 1.5 Miles

"Have I not commanded you? Be strong and courageous; do not be afraid, nor be dismayed, for the Lord your God is with you wherever you go."

—Joshua 1:9

I slept in today for the first time. Yep, getting up at 7:30 a.m. was really nice. I realized today I was skipping several stages of my journey, but I had to stay focused on the fact that I was still able to walk. If I had any chance of making it to Santiago, it would only be if I came to terms with my unknown illness and manage it as best I could.

I still hadn't figured out the bus route, so I knew I had to get back over there and see if I could find some help. I needed to figure out how to get to Baamonde. My revised walking plan would have to restart at Baamonde because that would fall into the hundred-kilometer distance to Santiago. *Once I get myself to that promised land, I can make it with the grace of my Lord.* I paid my outrageous bill of forty-five euros for my room and dinner last night. I shouldn't complain; it was very well worth it. I was just trying to be tight so I would not run out of money. I walked to the bus station without worry, although my feet were very worried, because I knew where it was (pat on the back).

As I was trying to figure out the schedule again, a gentleman approached me and asked if he could be of assistance. He introduced himself as Antonio and said that he was a taxi driver. I introduced myself and graciously accepted his help. I informed him I needed to get to Baamonde but couldn't see a direct ticket from Ribadeo. He informed me that it was because there were no buses that went to Baamonde from there. I would have to take a bus to Foz, and from Foz I could get on a bus to Baamonde. Great! At last! That's what I needed help with. I would have never figured it out. Thank you, Lord. I would have never figured out Foz because it was way out of my direction.

He asked me where I was from, and of course I blurted, "Texas," with great pride. We continued to converse as we walked right into the bar attached to the bus station. He offered to buy me a coffee, but I already had a Coke Zero I was enjoying. I purchased a croissant, and we sat down and continued our pleasant conversation. We enjoyed our quick breakfast, and before he left, I thanked him again for resolving my confusion and prayed he would have a blessed day. He smiled fondly and walked back to his taxi.

I walked out to the benches where the buses came to park for loading and unloading. I found a convenient one to where the bus I was supposed to jump on would be parking. While I was waiting, a mother and daughter approached and sat right next to me. It didn't take any time for me to break the ice and greet them. I introduced myself and asked permission to ask her a question. Of course, my question was if they were going to Foz. She responded with a yes and then introduced them to me. Mom's name was Marisol, and her nine-year-old daughter was Alba. I asked her if she wouldn't mind helping me out with my trip, as I could not read Spanish and they normally don't announce where the bus is stopping. Marisol was more than happy to help me out. She began asking me the regular questions, and when I responded with "Texas," that darling little girl couldn't take her eyes off of me. Sometimes these sweet little angels make me feel like I'm just so super strange or I'm a celebrity, not sure which. The bus came within a short while, and we all found our seats. Of course, Marisol and Alba sat right across the aisle from me just like guardian angels.

During this lengthy bus ride, I found myself getting emotional because I just couldn't figure out why things weren't working out for me like I had originally planned. I didn't understand why all these things were happening to me—dealing with all this pain, getting lost, and now venturing way off the Camino only to try to figure out how to get back on it. I lost a lot of miles going on the detour, but I just had to focus on making it those last kilometers with the feet I have attached to this old body. *I just have to depend on this incredible amount of faith I have in my Lord Jesus to help guide me and get me where I need to be.* I prayed so very hard and diligently, begging my Savior to help me keep putting one foot in front of the other and in the right direction. *It appears to me that he keeps sending me angels to assist me in every way they can, so I must continue on with my faith for all the miracles he has thrown my way.*

Upon arrival to Foz, Marisol and Alba offered me a pastry prior to unloading. These pastries were in one of the fanciest boxes I've ever seen pastries stored in. It was gift-wrapped, so I thought for sure it was for someone special. But Marisol opened it, and when I saw them, they looked awfully expensive, and I didn't want them to feel obligated to offer me one, so at first I just said no thank you. Marisol would not have it. She insisted I try one of the best pastries Spain had to offer. Alba as well was encouraging me to try one, stating they were her favorites. To appease them, I accepted, and it made both of them utterly happy. Sure enough, they were telling the absolute truth. Best flaky, melt-in-your-mouth pastry I've ever had in Spain. Not sure if I've had another to compare to, but this one was up there. I thanked them graciously and told them it was definitely delicious. We said our goodbyes and parted ways. Alba was still staring at me with a smile.

The bus schedule posted in Foz was just as confusing as the one in Ribadeo. I really needed to learn how to read Spanish. I quickly asked a stranger standing next to me, and she provided reassurance of the bus I thought I was supposed to get on for Baamonde. Apparently every bus station has a bar, and this one was no different. I was hungry anyway, so I ordered a hamburger. Unfortunately, the bartender informed me that they were out of hamburger meat but that they could make me a bacon sandwich. I nodded okay, and a short while later, they delivered. What a mistake! It cost twelve euros! And that was just the sandwich! Not worth bragging about either. *Oh well, I won't be back this direction anyway.*

The bus was running ten minutes late, but eventually I got on, and it was the right one. I prayed again that I would get off at the right stop in Baamonde. I did without worry, and what was even more delightful was that the albergue was half a block from the bus stop. Thank you, Lord.

This albergue had washing machines, so I caught up on my laundry and then walked to the Supermercado (Supermarket) to fill up on snacks in preparation for my continued walk. I noticed many people watching me, several of whom stopped and asked me if they could help me. It was probably because I was walking like I was eighty years old. I just said, "I have bad feet," in Spanish, smiled, and carried on. Sometimes I was embarrassed at drawing so much attention. The ibuprofen did wonders, but tonight my ankles were really swollen even after not walking much for the past two days. This albergue was really beautiful with lots of wood. It even had a gorgeous fireplace where pilgrims gathered to mingle and share their stories. I visited very little here and retired early after my usual routine. Prayers ended my day with great thankfulness to my dear God. I prayed hard that I would make it to Santiago. *Now I lay me down to sleep.*

CHAPTER 30

Day 18: September 8th, Baamonde to Miraz - 9 Miles

But those who wait on the LORD Shall renew their strength; They shall mount up with wings like eagles, They shall run and not be weary, They shall walk and not faint.

—Isaiah 40:31

My nerves got the best of me. I didn't sleep well, worried about if I could make it nine miles to my next destination. I got up about 6:20 a.m. for an early start—quietly of course, as everyone else was still sleeping. I love it when I have a community bathroom all to myself. I really tried to enjoy my walk, and I did for the most part. I took lots of pictures, listened to music, admired the countryside, and said, "Buen Camino," to many pilgrims. It was really nice. It took me almost six hours to walk nine miles to get to Miraz, but I made it! It was the pace I could handle. Oh thank you, Jesus!

Miraz

The albergue wasn't open yet, so of course I found my way to the local bar. This town was extremely small but so very lovely. As I was enjoying my beer and pincho outside on the patio, one of my pilgrim friends I had met last night, Wolfgang from Austria, walked up with his daughter, Sara. I asked them to join me. Gladly they did, and we chatted like monkeys. Well, Wolfgang and I did—Sara, not so much. She appeared a little withdrawn. While Wolfgang went to relieve himself, Sara informed me that she had been on the Camino for the previous two weeks and that her father had just joined her to walk the last week together. I thought that was so cool, to do a father/daughter walk together. She said he talked too much. I laughed. They had slept at the same albergue I did the night before, and they actually passed me several times. Everybody passed me several times. What can I say? When Wolfgang returned, he informed me that he was a physiotherapist and would like to work on my feet after we checked into the albergue, if I allowed him to.

"Of course, that would be awesome," I gladly replied.

Now it was Sara's turn to take a break. She went into the bar. While she was absent, Wolfgang informed me that although he was a strong believer in God, Sara, on the other hand, was not a believer. It didn't surprise me anymore, and I told Wolfgang that I had met many nonbelievers on the Camino. I told him it was a good thing that she was there, perhaps to find answers like the others. He was skeptical but was very glad they were spending time together. He reassured me he was a strong believer and wished he could do something that would change her thinking. I told him I would share a story with her about the morning I woke up and couldn't walk, how within a couple of hours I was walking. I did share that story with her upon her return, in hopes that I could serve as a testimony to divine intervention. I told her I had no idea what was wrong with my feet. They were painful, swollen, and wanted to give up with every step, but with my strong belief in his existence, I kept going. She agreed that something was wrong, as she witnessed me walking several times. I told her I wasn't going to give up as long as I had God on my side. She nodded but not convincingly.

While waiting for the albergue to open, I got to enjoy one of the coolest things I've ever seen in a town. A lady was coming toward the bar down the street with all her cows. Not just one or two cows but a whole herd of beautiful brown and white cows. I had to go stand right on the edge of the street as they were passing by like it was a parade. I petted one or two of them as they passed. It was so enjoyable that these cows were just following this lady. They didn't venture off down another street, but one did stop momentarily right in front of me to nibble on some grass. They were just walking by like they owned this town. Come to find out, they practically do! A customer said they pass by once in the morning to go feed out at pasture and return home with their owner later in the day. Wow, can you image having so many pet cows? Lucky lady. For some bizarre reason, I wasn't afraid of them anymore. Cool.

This same gentleman who was explaining the cows after they passed started asking me questions about where I was from. This guy got so excited when I said, "Texas." He said he knew where Austin was!

He was so thrilled that he was meeting me and told me to stay right there at that bar, that he would be back in a second. I complied, and upon his return, he was wearing a Texas Longhorn T-shirt and an American bandana with the biggest smile on his face. He was just so proud of showing off his T-shirt. I just laughed so hard and told him all about my family that lives in Austin. We conversed for at least an hour, and by then, the albergue was open.

The albergue was super cool. I really enjoyed this one. After checking into my bunk and unpacking, I went out to the garden to visit with whoever was out there. Sure enough, Wolfgang was at one of the tables waiting for me. He was telling me about his business in his country and that he did therapy for lots of reasons, mostly pain. I was only wearing my sandals, so he started doing pressure point massaging on my feet. He then moved up to my calves and behind my knees. That was actually more painful than my original pain, but when I went walking, it wasn't quite as painful. It actually worked! My gait even changed for a few minutes. The pain eventually returned, but at least it was relieved for a short while. What a sweet angel this man was. He really wanted to make me feel better.

We visited a bit longer with other pilgrims, and then I went to visit the hospitalero. He spoke very good English because these volunteers were from the British Confraternity of Saint James. I asked him where the local church was because I wanted to go visit it and say a prayer. He informed me that it was locked, but if I waited until 7:00 p.m., he would meet me there and unlock it for me. He made me feel special. What a nice guy.

I ventured into the town to admire it and eventually made it to the church about an hour early. It was relatively small, as I expected. Miraz is a very small village, but they definitely have everything they need—a church, a bar, and cows. The church was encircled by a cemetery. I went all the way around, looking at tombstones and reading them. It was so enchanting. There was a huge tree on the front left side of the church with a bench, so I waited there listening to my music until the hospitalero showed up. We greeted, and he unlocked the church.

He started giving me a history of the church and how proud the town's people were of it. He said it was built in the eleventh century. The wooden relic behind the altar was made three hundred years ago, around 1717. He shared with me that St. James was on both sides of the cross of Jesus. On one of the carved relics of St. James, he was on a horse, and there were two bloody heads at the horse's feet. He explained that this one is "St. James the Moor killer." I came to understand that this was one of St. James's two faces. Rumor has it that at the Battle of Clavijo, St. James appeared (well after his death) on a white horse and led them into battle against the Muslim forces, eventually winning that battle. On the other side was Santiago Peregrino, his pilgrim identity. This is the one I see most often. He is standing with his staff and scallop shell. He pointed to two large bricks at the lower end of the side wall and stated those were the only two original bricks. The rest of the church has been kept up through the years with necessary reconstruction. I thanked him for taking the time to spend with me and educating me. That was very kind of him.

I lit a candle and said a prayer. *Thank you, God, for giving me this spectacular opportunity. I am so very blessed.* I made it back to the albergue with moderate but tolerable pain. I received a very special text from my daughter Gina. She made me feel so good I bought her a green T-shirt from the hospitalero to commemorate. I slipped into my sleeping bag after my routine and kept smiling well into my dreams. Amen.

CHAPTER 31

Day 19: September 9th, Miraz to Roxica - 8.8 Miles

> Is anyone among you sick? Let him call for the elders of the church, and let them pray over him, anointing him with oil in the name of the Lord.
>
> —James 5:14

I slept in just a little. I didn't leave until 8:00 a.m. because I knew I was only going to walk about eight or nine miles. I woke up happy because of my daughter's text just letting me know how proud she was of me. I had bought that T-shirt for her but knew I couldn't buy any more gifts until after my arrival to Santiago, if indeed I made it. I had no room in my backpack and had to refrain from so many tempting items I had wanted to buy.

My enjoyable walk to Roxica went fairly well. My pain level was moderate but more severe on my left foot. I found that once in a while if I stopped and picked up one foot, rotated it around several times, and got the circulation stimulated, it really helped. So this prolonged my arrival to Roxica, but at least I made it. *Thank you,*

God, for watching over me. Thank you for helping me to walk and guiding me in the right direction.

I made it to my next destination by about one or two o'clock. I found Casa Roxica and met Elena, the angel that runs this albergue. She only houses six pilgrims, as it is out of her home and kind of in the middle of nowhere. I was sitting outside on a lawn chair while Elena was still cleaning from the previous night's stay. Two other hikers approached, asking if this was an albergue. I informed them it was indeed but that the owner was still cleaning the room and beds. They sat down and introduced themselves. They were a lovely lesbian couple from I'm guessing England, on account of their accent. I remember their unique hair. It looked like a rat's nest, those stylish dreadlocks. I thought, *They are on the Camino. Who cares if you go weeks without washing your hair?* I was only doing mine once a week, but that is my usual even at home.

Elena had offered me a beer, so I was sipping it while visiting with these two new friends. I told them about the time I got lost and how I ended up having the most incredible meal of a lifetime. They were so touched by my story. I was so glad that I could share it with them as a testament to my Savior, my Lord God, the Almighty. The girls decided not to stay and continued their journey. I would run into them a few more times to share some memories and laughter.

Elena came back out with a bowl of some concoction. It was a type of oil that smelled like rubbing alcohol. She placed it next to my feet, as I had already removed my boots, and she placed my left foot in the bowl. I was trying to tell her that it wasn't necessary as she was starting to rub my foot and ankle. But she insisted that it would make me feel much better. I was so apologetic and told her I felt bad that she was doing this for me. She just continued explaining that she wanted to do this, it made her happy, and for me to just relax. I couldn't relax. I didn't know how. I felt so unworthy. She was making my feet feel so much better, and I was suddenly taken back to my church, growing up in Farmington. "Lord, I am not worthy to receive you, but only say the word, and I shall be healed." I kept repeating that to myself. Elena was so content rubbing my swollen feet, but I just couldn't help but feel bad that she felt this sorry for me. *Lord, please forgive me and please bless Miss Elena. Thank you for this angel.* I couldn't believe how much better this alcohol or oil or whatever it was made my feet feel. It was miraculous. *I don't know why, Lord, you have blessed me with so many angels, but thank you, thank you, thank you endlessly. I shall always serve you.* When she finished, she showed me to the room, and I selected my bunk.

I took my shower, prepared for the next day's hike, listened to my music while I Facebooked, and took a nap before dinner. Of course I devoured it. A mixture of chicken and potatoes, a salad, and plenty of wine along with pleasant conversations with just a handful of pilgrims. Elena's place fills up fast for those who can't make it to the next major town or the ones like me who can only walk limited miles per day.

There was an older couple walking together, and when we were winding down for the evening in our room, he was complaining to his wife about how badly his feet hurt. I got out of my sleeping bag and dug into my backpack to get the cream that sweet soccer player in Columba gave to me. I limped over to their bunks and told him it was a gift and that it had helped me on several nights. I told him it was an anti-inflammatory and that I had plenty of other regiments, so he gladly accepted my gift. They both thanked me, and I crawled back into my sanctuary of prayers. *Thank you, God, for helping me help others. Thank you for Elena.*

CHAPTER 32

Day 20: September 10th, Roxica to Sobrado dos Monxes - 13.5 Miles

---

"For where two or three are gathered together in My name, I am there in the midst of them."
—Matthew 18:20

Today was a truly enjoyable six-and-a-half-hour walk. With my heaven-sent crutches, my high spirits, my infinitely growing faith, I so enjoyed every minute. My feet were behaving for the most part but still letting me know they weren't right. My left heel for the past several days has been much more painful than the right for some reason. My ibuprofen was on board, and my camera did not cease from clicking all day long. It was simply that beautiful.

I embraced and absorbed all the morning noises—chickens, birds, frogs, cows, it was all so nice. The trails were pleasant as well, not muddy or challenging, and no one passed me for several hours. The first one who did just so happened to be the gentleman I had given the anti-inflammatory cream to. He was walking alone, so after I said good morning, I asked him where his wife was. He replied he left her at the bar where they had breakfast, and she was taking her time. She would catch up to him at the next town. I was really surprised that they weren't walking together.

When I finally made it to O Mesón, I stopped for lunch at the local bar, and this old man's wife walked in. We greeted, and she asked the server if they had orange juice. It was a negative, so she turned angrily around and walked out in a frumpy kind of way. Every morning, you wake up with a choice of what kind of day you are going to have. Your attitude paves the way. *Perhaps her husband had something to do with it*, I thought to myself. I paid for lunch and continued this most delightful hike.

I was so excited to be going to Sobrado dos Monxes because I would be staying in the monastery Monasterio de Santa Maria de Sobrado, which was founded in 952 AD. The older couple and I had a conversation at dinner regarding the monastery, and they both voted against staying there. They had decided to stay at the Albergue Lecer, as they had been told it was much nicer and it was only eight euros. The monastery was six euros, and as far as I was concerned, nice or not, it was an absolute privilege to have the opportunity to stay there. Why would I want to stay anywhere else?

As I was entering the town, I could see the steeples of the cathedral, and it was so exciting. I was so anxious to get there that it took away from my feet the attention they were seeking. *I know, I know, I'll give you rest shortly; just get me there first. Thank you Lord, thank you for seeing me through this. Please help me make it.*

Monastery

The monastery did not open until 4:30 p.m., so I had plenty of time to go find a bank, as I was running low on cash. I also needed to find a pharmacy and a grocery store to stock up. Unbelievably, every single store I needed was right there across the street from the church. *How do I keep getting so lucky?* I looked up to the sky, kissed my fingers, and gave a peace sign to my Lord. I love you, Jesus!

I went back across the street and into the bar that was right in front of the church. After ordering a beer, I quickly recognized the sixty-six-year-old man, Karl, who had been walking for three months from Wren, Austria.

We made eye contact, and I said, "Austria, right?"

He replied, "Yes," and it took him only a second to remember me. "Oh yes, Texas." He was absolutely amazed that I was still walking. He said he could not believe his eyes! I informed him that I had to revise my schedule in order to attempt to make it the last hundred kilometers. He understood immediately that I was concentrating on the Compostela.

He just kept shaking his head and asked me, "How are you still walking?"

I responded with, "By the grace of God. Truly, I don't have an answer for you except my faith. I'm amazed myself that one foot keeps stepping in front of the other!"

We laughed and enjoyed our conversation. I was still hurting with every step, but it was a tolerable pain that stayed well under some magical control.

I had met another pilgrim earlier that day, from Poland, who was studying astronomy. He sat next to me and the older gentleman. I wish I could remember his name; there were so many, and I usually wrote them down when I was journaling in the evening, but this one I missed.

So many more familiar faces started popping into the bar. I absolutely loved these reunions. Unexpected friendships developed on a daily basis. It was so beautiful. We all chatted until the monastery opened.

Once opened, the bar was practically emptied. I checked in, which was quite a different process. You got escorted to your room by one of the volunteers. Once in your room, you could then choose your bunk. I naturally grabbed the one on the bottom and close to an electrical outlet. After unpacking, I went exploring this outrageous, most incredible monastery. I felt so privileged to get to spend the night there. I can't even describe it. I went into the church and took so many pictures. I marveled at this religious mansion. The high ceilings, the paintings, the statues, the layout, just everything. I was so intrigued I got lost in my bewilderment. This place was ancient and had so much history. I was told by one of the volunteers that even John the Baptist had a chapel there built in the pre-Cistercian history. Incredible. This was a dream.

I reminisced around the yard and hallways and then went back to the bar for dinner. They actually had paella on the menu and seafood paella at that! I love this dish and couldn't believe this was the first time I ran into it. Naturally, I ordered it and asked the bartender why I hadn't seen it before, as I thought it was a popular Spain specialty. He stated it was more popular in southern Spain and not so much the north.

I hurried up and finished dinner because I wanted to make it to the 7:00 p.m. mass where, I was informed, the monks would be singing. I had a little trouble finding the location in this massive puzzle of a monastery, so by the time I found it, I was late. I walked in quietly and sat down by one of my pilgrim friends. What I found so interesting is I thought it was going to be a typical Catholic mass where the priest said his sermon, and then the monks were going to sing on cue. I was totally wrong. This was the authentic Roman Catholic tradition of monks singing the entire mass. I didn't understand the language, and I'd never attended anything like this, but I remember seeing it on TV as a child. I think it was in the Vatican around Christmas time. It didn't sound Spanish or French. Perhaps Latin? So interesting. Unfortunately, I only stayed about thirty minutes because I was exhausted and had started to doze off. I slipped out just as quietly as I snuck in.

I made it back to my room, heavily prayed, and happily retired from this most spectacular day. This place was amazing.

CHAPTER 33

Day 21: September 11th, Sobrado dos Monxes to Boimorto - 8.8 Miles

> Every good gift and every perfect gift is from above, and comes down from the Father of lights, with whom there is no variation or shadow of turning.
>
> —James 1:17

I woke up feeling so blessed. How fortunate to be able to stay in this magnificent house of our Lord. The only possible way is with your passport. You must be a pilgrim. This hike truly has its benefits. My feet were behaving, as they had been accustomed to doing in the mornings, with mild to moderate pain. I continued my ibuprofen, putting my boots on before attempting to walk. I rubbed them at night before bed but mostly prayed for them and believed in him. Thus far, it had been an extraordinary experience, and I thanked the good Lord for allowing me to walk every day. I had explored the church and all the chapels the day before and was still in awe.

Leaving that morning, I turned around and admired it one last time. *Thank you, God, for this privilege.*

I wasn't absolutely sure which way to leave the city. I had not looked for the arrows or shells the day before, probably because I was so enthralled by the church I simply forgot. Since I wasn't absolutely sure, I decided I would look for another pilgrim and just follow them out of the city. Mind you, it was still a little dark, so the shadows were displayed from the streetlights. I caught a glimpse of a shadow, certain it was another pilgrim. I decided to follow it and suddenly realized it was my own. Leave it to me, but it was okay because when I reached the main street, there were several pilgrims finishing their morning coffee and breakfast. Most all of them were heading west, so I just followed until I found my first shell. By that time, they were all well ahead of me. I had to stop and take a picture of this shell because it was so beautiful. It was made entirely of gold.

It was 54°F this morning, one of the colder mornings on this journey. I was fairly warm, except for my fingers. My thumbs actually went numb, and I couldn't feel them for a good while. It took about an hour before it finally started warming up and my thumbs started getting some feeling back. So many familiar faces were passing me. All these wonderful pilgrims would say they were praying for me and then would tell me to go slowly. I complied and thanked each one for their concern. It was such a privilege to be a part of this heavenly family. I knew today I was only going to make it to Boimorto.

A girl from Poland named Justine, slowed down to walk with me for several kilometers. We had a very engaging conversation. She was asking me a zillion questions. She was so interested in me for some reason, so I kept her entertained. I told her about my children, my failed marriages, my miraculous experiences on the Camino, and my wonderful boyfriend God has blessed me with. She was going to get married last June and called it off because it just wasn't feeling right. I told her that it was a good thing and that she must feel 100 percent sure before she made such a huge life decision. I told her everything happens for a reason, and sometimes it takes a long time to figure it out. Sometimes you never do, but there is a reason out there somewhere. She said calling off the wedding was the reason she was on the Camino, to find peace, be with nature, and figure things out. I told her there is no better place to be to try to figure things out, as long as you allow God to be a part of your walk. The Camino has its way of doing that to each and every pilgrim. We talked of numerous other subjects before we stopped at the bar in As Corredoiras.

There were several familiar faces taking a break out on the patio and even more inside. I ordered a coffee and quick snack and joined my friend I had been visiting with. Two other girls joined us. The gentleman who kept leaving his wife behind was inside. He had started a conversation with me, but he was that kind that never ceases enjoying hearing himself talk, so I kindly excused myself and told him I had friends outside waiting for me. Moments after I sat down outside, he came running, yelling at me to come back inside, saying there was important news on the TV. Why he focused on me more than the others, I could not understand. So I motioned to the other girls to come with me. Apparently, there was a missing female pilgrim from the United States who was walking on the Camino Francés. She had been missing since the evening before, and there had been an extensive search by all authorities. That explained why he wanted me to listen, as I was the only one from the US. I kept thinking to myself, *And you want me to listen to this because?* I didn't want to hear that kind of news. I always felt so very safe and looked after by my Lord. I certainly didn't need this news at the moment, but I did say a quick prayer for her safety, and then I walked back outside to enjoy my coffee.

I decided that I really like coffee with Baileys. I'd never been a coffee drinker until Spain. Baileys with coffee was certainly something I wanted to continue at home. It never crossed my mind to utilize it as a creamer. Pretty scrumptious. Of course only one will do. More than that would give me an early-morning buzz. Come to think about it, I don't think I ever caught a buzz on my trip. I usually maxed out at two beers, and I was done. It reminded me of my Jay. He is definitely a two-drink-only kind of guy. I really like that about him.

I finished up some more talk with other pilgrims and then took off. I only had about two more miles to go. One lady I had visited with at the last bar caught up to me and saw that I was still limping along with my crutches. She suggested that I place some feminine napkins inside my shoes to soften my steps. I thought this was the funniest suggestion I'd received thus far on my walk. She offered to give me a couple, and I thanked her for her kindness but informed her that I had already purchased Dr. Scholl's liners, and they were in my shoes. I told her she was so very sweet, I appreciated her greatly, and that I would pray for her.

I arrived at the albergue in Boimorto at 11:30 a.m., and of course I was the only one there. There was a sign on the door that said it didn't open until 1:00 p.m. and to call the number posted. I walked around the place and took in the scenery. There was a pond close by, and I admired the wildlife and flowers. Nature is so naturally beautiful. It doesn't even have to try; God just made her that way. I lay down on one of the metal benches they had outside and just rested, listened to my classic rock, and had a great conversation with God. *Today has been so lovely. Thank you, Lord, for helping me get here. Thank you for protecting me.*

At 12:30 p.m., I called the number, and the lady said she would be there to open up at 1:00 p.m. She was right on time, but I noticed nobody else was. No other pilgrims had stopped, so I figured this wasn't a common stop, and perhaps that's why they have you call the number. If no calls, they simply don't bother opening it up. It was a very nice, more modern type of albergue. The décor was more upscale than all the other albergues I had stayed in. The kitchen had stainless steel appliances, and the washroom was fairly modernized as well. It didn't cost any more than the usual, but I was really surprised no other pilgrims had checked in.

Apparently this midsize town was having a major fiesta, and

the rooms were going to be occupied by many out-of-towners. Every bed eventually got filled up by mid-afternoon. The lady that ran this joint kept me updated and told me it might get a little loud that night, as it was definitely going to be a party. *Wonderful*, I thought. *I love parties.*

I went walking into the town to discover its pleasantries, enjoy a beer, obtain some stamps, and look for tomorrow's arrows. I found them fairly easily. Of course I was getting all kinds of "oh poor girl" looks from people passing me by, due to my inability to walk normally and the dependency of my walking sticks. I was hurting, but I could tolerate it enough to enjoy the town. I found the church, but it was locked, so I just ventured around it and then headed back to the main drag.

My tummy started rumbling, so I figured I would go find a nice restaurant and eat a delicious dinner, even though it was still kind of early for Spain standards. Villanova Restauranté looked exclusive, so I selected that one and entered. Very few patrons were in there, so I knew it was early. I sat down and was entertained by the menu alone. Their Menu del Dia had several choices, and since rabbit was one of them, I elected to try it. Never in my life had I tried rabbit. This was exciting. So very glad I tried it; not only was it delicious, it went very well with wine! That was a first.

I made it back to the albergue with God's assistance, showered, and crawled into my bag by about eight o'clock to relieve my swollen feet. At 8:45 p.m., Maricele, the hospitalera, asked me if I would kindly come and visit with her daughter Sheila. Maricele was so excited to be hosting a real Texan and had been telling her daughter all about me. I obliged with a smile and dragged my happy self out of my warm sleeping bag to go visit in the living room. There were several couches with lots of people visiting. Sheila and I met, sat down, and had an extremely lengthy conversation. Come to find out Maricele really wanted me to come talk to her so that her daughter could practice her English. You see, Sheila was attending the university in Santiago, majoring in language arts, with English being her focus. She did speak rather well, and I only corrected her a few times. We exchanged contact information because she wanted me to call her if and when I arrived in Santiago. She would be back in class by then. This girl was so beautiful. I was captivated by her jet-black hair, flawless skin, and gorgeous smile. Simply beautiful and intelligent. I can understand why her mother was so very proud.

I kept her entertained for about two hours and ended our tutoring session at 10:30 p.m. I crawled back to bed, but I could not go to sleep because all the party animals had arrived and continued the fiesta in the dining area. The music was blaring, the laughter was louder, and the noise was not going to cease anytime soon. I was getting aggravated but realized that if I had not been hurting so much or been so tired, I would have gone and joined the party. Unfortunately, my body was not in party mode, so I just prayed, Facebooked, wrote, listened to my—no wait, their—music, and prayed that I wouldn't be kept up until wee hours of the morning. This was the first albergue that didn't have a mandatory "lights out at ten" curfew. Eventually, shortly after midnight, the music started slowing down, as well as the noise in general. People started retiring for the night, and soon enough, everyone went to sleep, including me.

CHAPTER 34

Day 22: September 12th, Boimorto to Arzúa - 9.5 Miles

"For if you forgive men their trespasses, your heavenly Father will also forgive you. But if you do not forgive men their trespasses neither will your Father forgive your trespasses."

—Matthew 6:14–15

When I woke up, it crossed my mind to pay them all back by making lots of noise, but that sounded way too evil. How dare I even entertain such a thought. I slept in a little longer and at seven got out of bed and prepared for the day as quietly as possible. I packed up and was so happy to be leaving, still a little resentful from last night's experience. Forgive and forget. Sometimes it's easier said than done, but I did forgive and didn't think about it again.

I walked through the town feeling really confident about knowing my way out. It was a charming, misty gray morning, but a heavy kind of mist, so I had to put on my rain poncho. I actually had to wear it most of the day. Even so, the paths and trails were stunningly beautiful. My feet were tolerable, as they had been holding on to about a four-to-six pain level, but they didn't stop me from absorbing all the sights, sounds, and smells of Spain. Another enchanting hike through this magical kingdom.

Four to five hours of walking would get me to Arzúa, and I spent the vast majority of it having long conversations with God and my dad. I sang him thankful praises for all he has done for me. For lifting me up and helping me walk. For keeping my pain level under a manageable control. For keeping me safe and watching over me. I was so occupied in prayer I didn't even realize that I had been carrying my crutches instead of using them. About four or five miles into my walk, my left heel started acting up and burning, so I stopped, rested just a bit, rotated my ankle for circulation, and started utilizing the crutches God sent to me. I slowed my pace down halfway to my next destination and even more so as I passed churches. I tried to open the door of each splendid church, but the majority of them were locked. Those that were opened, I would enter, say a prayer, and if available retrieve a stamp, evidence that I had been there.

As I entered Arzúa, I noticed there were a lot more choices of albergues to stay at. The Northern Route had merged with the Francés Route several towns ago, and therefore the number of pilgrims had multiplied. Plus, it was getting closer to Santiago.

I was looking for this particular albergue that I had chosen to stay in during my walk, out of my guidebook. The directions instructed me to take a left at the "T" on top of the hill after I passed the *"poliodeportivo,"* but I had no idea what that word meant. This city was relatively quiet, but I ran into a nice lady who was walking with her child to soccer practice. It was kind of obvious, as he was in uniform and carrying his prize possession. I showed her the word in my book and asked her what that meant. She pointed to the soccer field she was taking her son to and stated in Spanish more directions that simply just got me more confused. I smiled and thanked her for her kindness and her time, not letting her know how jumbled she got my brain. So after they departed, I resorted to Google Maps. Thank you, Lord, for Google Maps! This city had internet service, so I utilized it to my benefit and found the albergue I was looking for. It was only 11:30 a.m. by now, but I had been walking for a good four hours, and my feet were talking to me, so I knew this was where I had to stay.

Without effort, I found a nearby bar and relaxed for a while. I obtained a stamp and then went to the nearby church to visit and take pictures. When I returned to the albergue, it was 12:20 p.m., and still no one was in sight. So I decided to just sit down and be first in line. I enjoyed my rest, my prayers, my music, and my time.

As it got closer to being opened, I recognized Dave walking toward me from down the cobblestone street, carrying his big guitar on his back. I heard him yell, "Is that Marissa?"

I waved as he approached, and upon arrival, we hugged. He kept saying how amazed he was to even see me.

"I can't believe you're still walking!" he proclaimed.

I told him that I had to come to terms with my issues and readjusted my itinerary so that I could make it the last hundred kilometers. I told him about my bus ride and the angels I met along the way. He was so happy to still see me on the trail and kept stressing his amazement. I don't know why I was not amazed; perhaps because I knew it was due to my dependency on and belief in the unseen. We conversed until the albergue opened and then claimed our beds for the night.

I was fortunate to be one of the first so that I could retreat to a bottom bunk. At this point, I couldn't imagine trying to climb up to a top bunk. I only had to do that two or three times on this trip, but it was relatively early in the journey before I started having feet issues.

I showered, washed all my clothes, and was so happy to get that chore done. I was really starting to smell. When you can smell yourself, you know it's bad. After a short nap, I went to find a

Chinese store where they sell electronics so I could buy a new phone charger. I managed to find myself back at the local bar and had paella again for dinner. I also enjoyed flan for dessert, along with Baileys and coffee. Although I was thoroughly enjoying myself, my feet really ached making it back to the albergue. They were swollen by now, so I rubbed them with my potions that I had been blessed with. I popped a couple of ibuprofen and said lots of prayers.

I prayed really hard, apprehensive about tomorrow's walk. I knew that it would be my longest attempt of the few days I had left on this journey. I followed through with my rituals, and when I was Facebooking, I saw that my sister-in-law, Sylvia, had posted to all her prayer warriors on Facebook to pray for me—to pray that I made it another day and to continue praying that I made this entire journey. That meant so much to me. The sudden calmness that took me over when I read her post was so unexpected. I knew now that God not only was going to help me make it, but that he had organized through Sylvia, a selection of angel cheerleaders, cheering me on, and that I had nothing to fear. *I can do this. I can do this and I will because God and all his angels will be with me. I am so very blessed. Thank you, Sylvia. Thank you, God.*

CHAPTER 35

Day 23: September 13th, Arzúa to Santa Irene - 12.2 Miles

For here we have no continuing city, but we seek the one to come.

—Hebrew 13:14

I hate it when you want to sleep in and your internal alarm goes off. I lay there at 6:00 a.m. thinking and praying, praying and thinking. *I'll sleep in a little more.* Pilgrims just seem more excited as you get closer to Santiago, and the enthusiasm affects their ability to sleep in just a little bit longer. It was way too much noise from other excited pilgrims, so I had to get up and start my day.

I got dressed, packed, and by seven I was ready to get back on the Camino. As I was rolling up my sleeping bag, a German girl who was conversing with me let me know that she walked at least twenty-two miles per day. She stated that she had already done the Camino de Francés, and it only took her twenty-three days. She was tall and slender and at the most twenty-five years of age, probably younger. I didn't know how to interpret this little *tuttie fruitie*. Was she bragging? Sounded like bragging to me.

I thought to myself, *Yeah? Let me see you do it thirty years from now, little girly. Let me see if you're still bragging then.*

I found myself getting a little resentful. *Push it aside, Marissa.* I smiled and replied, "Wow, that's impressive."

I told her I was taking my sweet time so that I could smell the roses, listen to the roosters, and jump over cow turds. I let her know I was enjoying my slow, sweet, and spiritual walk. Each to his own; be respectful. Someday, she too will slow down. What I thought was really funny was that well into my walk, I passed her by as she was taking a smoke break! If I was able to pass her, that could only mean … how many smoke breaks? *Oh yes, my dear, thirty years from now.* Then I really laughed!

I had to wear my poncho practically all day. It rained almost nonstop. My boots and socks were wet, but at least my feet didn't hurt too badly—just a little, and I could handle it well. I had been trying to wean myself off the ibuprofen and was now down to only twice a day instead of every six hours. I stopped for a Baileys and coffee at A Calzada at about nine. The trails, even in the rain, were just so enchanting. At times I felt like I was in a storybook setting.

I continued taking pictures of this perplexing and bewildering country. My prayers were nonstop, both of thankfulness and asking for mercy. I so badly wanted to make it to Santiago. I wanted so badly to pay homage to St. James. I wanted to touch his statue and pray over his ashes. *This never even crossed my mind while I was planning and preparing for my trip over a year ago, but somehow that is how it is ending. Was this your plan all along, Lord? If so, I will do all in my power and yours to complete it. Have mercy on me.*

I made it to the albergue by 12:30. This one opened at 1:00 p.m., so I didn't have long to wait. So many pilgrims passed me right on by. I must have said, "Buen Camino," at least a hundred times. Not a soul stopped to stay at this albergue that was right on the trail in this quaint and silent town. I was not going to push it; I listened to my feet very diligently.

When the albergue opened, I selected my bunk and took a nap. After my shower and unpacking, I was walking back to the nearby bar, which was only about half a kilometer away, when I ran into my two lesbian friends sitting in a shelter, waiting out the rain. Even though it was just a sprinkle, they were still sitting there chatting and singing, just really happy people. When they recognized me passing by, they yelled to me, and I gladly went to join them and visit. They were so elated to see that I was still walking. We shared our stories and memories we had been creating during this unforgettable experience. They seemed so happy together. It really warms my heart when two people collide to make one. A true love partnership, just as love is supposed to be. Their mangled hairstyles had not changed. So amusing. They said they were going all the way to whatever town they mentioned, and I told them the only reason I had made it this far was because I had been listening to my feet and to God. Therefore, I was staying put for the night. We wrapped up our laughter and went our separate ways. God be with them.

After I devoured my delightful but very late lunch, I made it back to the albergue slowly but surely. I had been on my feet far too long, so I decided to call that dinner as well because I just wasn't going to make it one more time. I talked to Jay for a long time because there was a good connection at this place. I told him how much I missed him and Skipper, his dog. I couldn't wait to see them both, but even more so, I told him how badly I needed to see my children.

I missed my girls so very much and even cried several times thinking about them. I told Jay that I wanted nothing more than to see their beautiful faces when I arrived back at the airport in Corpus. He said he would do what it took to see that my wish was fulfilled. I love him so much.

It was still early evening when this small albergue was starting to fill up. A very young, blonde Russian girl plopped herself down on the bunk next to mine. I introduced myself, and she did as well. When she told me she was from Russia, I started asking many questions, as I think Russian is a fascinating country and only know what I have learned from textbooks and mandatory classes. She told me she hated her country and that she would someday figure out a way to escape it. The more I listened to her talk about her country, the more depressed I got for her sake. Maybe what I did learn in class was true. Communism is not that great from a social or individual standpoint. I've never met anyone who despised their country like this child. I answered all her questions regarding the States and let her know how fortunate I felt I was. I asked her questions about how she was able to get permission to walk the Camino and what she had to do to get here. She told me about all the red tape and how she was being watched and monitored, just as all Russians are when leaving their country for various reasons. I told her I would pray for her and hoped that someday she finds happiness. Now I felt guilty for being as happy as I am, even with my painful feet. *I am thankful for them, knowing I am free to walk wherever, whenever.* She really put lots of thoughts into my head about how very fortunate all of us are who don't live in those countries that are run by dictators. *Thank you, Jesus.* I did pray for her during my nightly prayers and routines well before I fell asleep and retired for the night.

CHAPTER 36

Day 24: September 14th, Santa Irene to Labacolla - 11.2 Miles

"But none of these things move me; nor do I count my life dear to myself, so that I may finish my race with joy, and the ministry which I received from the Lord Jesus, to testify to the gospel of the grace of God."

—Acts 20:24

Naturally, it was another morning of wishful thinking of sleeping in. Yeah, right! I estimated that it would take me only about four hours to make it to Labacolla, so I was in no hurry to get up. It was the other pilgrims making so much noise who enticed me to get moving, and thus I did. I said good morning to my Russian friend, and she responded, but it did not appear she was having a very happy morning. I knew her story now, so I didn't try to make small talk. I will continue to pray for her. I packed up my gear and was back out on the trail by 7:30 a.m.

This morning was another gray and gloomy, dark morning. The

fog was lingering thick while kissing the earth. It actually called for use of my Patrick Sharkathon headlamp. Shark Man would be proud.

It rained all day and stayed fairly dark, but with the grace of God, I did not get lost, nor was I in excruciating pain. It was there, but it was tolerable. I prayed to my Lord and kept thanking him, kept kissing my cross with every arrow and shell I encountered, kept listening to my music as I kept putting one foot in front of the other. I also kept smiling. I was so very happy knowing that tomorrow, if it be God's will, I would arrive in Santiago.

Most every pilgrim that passed me by today was walking all the way to Santiago. I knew what I could handle and therefore kept my slow and steady pace. After walking for four to five miles, my heels would start getting more anxious and let me know not to push it. As I was strolling through one of the little villages, I was surprised to see they actually had a couple of vending machines along the Camino. I hadn't eaten anything for breakfast because I had not passed any restaurants or bars, so I took advantage of what these machines had to offer. I selected a Coke Light and some chocolate chip cookies. Excellent choice.

About 9:30 a.m., I was passing a very populated bar where numerous pilgrims were having coffee and breakfast. I got lucky and grabbed a table that had just been vacated. I dumped my backpack and my sticks on the table and went and stood in line. When I asked the waiter for some Baileys with a shot of coffee, the lady behind me laughed out loud. Of course I was just kidding.

He said in Spanish, "Isn't it a bit early?"

I responded, "No, it's about 5:00 p.m. in Texas, so it's okay."

They both laughed. I went back to my table and enjoyed my beverage. The activity surrounding me was joyful, pilgrims coming and going, greeting each other with hugs and smiles. It was like Disneyland. Everyone should get to experience it at least once in their lifetime.

I rested long enough and joyfully jumped back on the trail,

continuing my travels and my prayers. Another shell, another sign, another arrow, another smile. I concentrated on talking to God most of today. I thanked him for everything again and again and again. I was so happy; my painful feet just couldn't keep me from smiling. My heart was so filled with joy.

When I entered the town of Labacolla, I thought about how peculiar the name was. My guidebook stated that it meant "wash scrotum." My Tex-Mex interpretation meant "wash your butt." I was instructed that it was one of the last stops before pilgrims reached Santiago, so they would bathe themselves there in the streams. I walked across a pedestrian bridge over one of those streams, but no one was taking a bath. The guidebook stated it was back in the Middle Ages. Now we have showers, albergues, and hotels. Yay.

I thought that following the path would take me right by the hotel where I had reserved a room. I kept looking for the Hotel Garcas, but I never saw it. I may not have been paying attention like I should have. I was admiring the flowers, the streams, and the people passing me. I completely missed it. When I got my GPS out, it stated I was nine minutes away if I followed the highway. I didn't want to follow the highway. I wanted to stay on the Camino and get to it off-road. So I kept going for another mile before I realized I had made a terrible mistake. It kept getting farther away according to my GPS, so I had to turn around and backtrack like I had done so many times before. This silliness added two more miles to my hike today. My feet were not happy.

I finally found my destination for the night and checked into the most extravagant room. This one was only thirty-three euros. What hard work and determination gets you sometimes is absolutely awesome. I rested my feet, showered, and later went to the hotel's restaurant to have dinner. The sweet waitress told me I could have dinner in the back in the quieter atmosphere, as compared to the crowded front. It also had a large window where you could enjoy the water's view. I gladly took her advice and thanked her kindly. I practically had the whole back area to myself.

When she told me they had fish and shrimp on the Menu del Dia, I almost couldn't contain myself. This was a special dinner for me, as it would be my last one on the Camino, for tomorrow, I should be arriving in Santiago de Compostela. Therefore, I would celebrate with fish and wine. This food was beyond description. Just when I thought I had already eaten the best meals ever, here comes this one and tops them all off. Unbelievable dinner! Thank you ever so much, Lord, for letting me experience this awesomeness. I wish I could have stolen their recipes to take home to Jay. He loves to cook, and he would have really enjoyed this dinner with me.

Somehow I got in touch with Marta and Kasia by phone, and they informed me they would make it to Santiago by the sixteenth. I promised I would be waiting for them and we would go have dinner together. They were so excited that I was still walking and that I was going to make it. Only by the grace of God would that happen, I told them.

I told the waitress to give my compliments to the chef and then ordered a Baileys to take back to the room with me. I completed all my nightly routines and rituals and just could not stop smiling. As I was settling in for the night, I realized that when I first started this journey, I had planned to do some creative writing, like some haiku poetry and just some simple poems, which I did. But tonight I realized that after that crucial morning when I could no longer stand, writing was no longer in the plan. I simply didn't realize that those creative juices stopped flowing, and all my thoughts and time were consumed with prayer. I realized on this final night that my original purpose, which was to go on an adventurous journey, somehow, on its own terms, became a spiritual one. I realized that every single day, my relationship with God became closer and closer. I know in my heart I would not have reached tonight without his constant presence. I truly always thought that I was spiritual, maybe not so religious, but certainly I considered myself spiritual. Well, this journey proved otherwise. You can never be close enough to God. Given the opportunity, placed in a situation where you have exhausted all options, there is always, every single time, a last resort … God! With faith and hope, his love will always pull you through. I was so incredibly happy because I believed that the following day, he was going to help me make it. At one point I was hopeless, and I now was in a place where I strongly felt I was going to succeed. I was going to walk into Santiago De Compostela sometime tomorrow! *Thank you, Lord, for that wonderful meal and this most wonderful day. Thank you for watching over me and carrying me through each and every day.*

CHAPTER 37

Day 25: September 15th, Labacolla to Santiago! - 8.8 Miles

Now may the God of hope fill you with all joy and peace in believing, that you may abound in hope by the power of the Holy Spirit.

—Romans 15:13

Naturally, I didn't sleep well. I was excited, nervous, and just a bit worried if my feet were going to give me any trouble. Therefore, I prayed from the moment I woke up. I prayed a lot. I wanted an early start but contemplated the amount of time I would be walking in the dark. I tried to go back to sleep, but it was useless, so I got up and started my day—of course with a smile.

I dressed, packed my bag, loaded up, and headed out. I stopped at the hotel's cafeteria for a quick snack, but this fella was so incredibly slow I changed my mind and walked across the street to the gasoline station. Nothing like a Coke Zero and cookies for breakfast, especially in a foreign country from a gas station.

It was still extremely dark. It was sometime between six thirty and seven, and it was rainy and windy. I had my poncho protecting me as much as possible, and I was wearing my headlight. This darkness was unlike the other mornings. What I found even more disturbing was the fact that there were no other pilgrims passing me by. It wasn't until about seven thirty that someone was approaching me from behind. It was still pitch dark, and I had flashbacks of that man who instructed me to go watch the TV regarding the murder. My prayers took over. My Lord was with me. I felt his presence. My fear started subsiding just as these footsteps were getting closer and closer.

Just as a silhouette passed me, I said in a squeaky voice, "Buen Camino!"

And a gentle voice responded, "Buen Camino," as he passed me.

I suddenly felt safe, just as before. Thank you, Jesus. Thank you for watching over me.

It had been a while since I saw the last arrow and started worrying if I had missed one. I stopped and looked around. Still, no other pilgrims. There were some houses, some woods, and some streetlights but no signs. Just like so many times before, I resorted to prayer. *Please, dear Lord, please show me a sign. I need some reassurance.* I continued on the straight path, and soon enough, the arrow came into sight, and I was relieved. I continued on the path as the dawn began to creep upon the asphalt. The wind had calmed, and the rain was now a drizzle.

It crossed my mind that I had to get two stamps today before I entered the city. I didn't start worrying about that dilemma until I encountered the first bar, which was closed. Would I not find one? *That just can't be. Goodness gracious, not here in Spain!* It still crossed my mind. I did encounter a bar in San Marcos and was able to obtain my first stamp for the day. I enjoyed my new favorite morning drink, Baileys and coffee.

> For the Lord will be your confidence, And will keep
> your foot from being caught.
> —Proverbs 3:26

I continued my glorious morning walk, my challenging hike, my adventurous travels, my spiritual journey, all rolled into one. I was elated when I encountered a church that was actually open. I went in, and sure enough, I was able to obtain my final stamp for my passport. How glorious that I would obtain my final stamp in a church. It just made me so happy. It was tiny, but just like any tiny church, it was a giant castle, a magnificent fortress, a spiritual palace. My feet had started to talk to me several miles earlier, but with prayer, I was able to tolerate and continue. I lit a candle and said a prayer. I noticed there were five candles already lit, and one was burned out. I knelt on the bench and went into a deep conversation with God. I started crying as I thanked him for constantly being with me. I thanked him for carrying me through my darkest moments—for showing me the way, not only with the signs but showing me the way into people's lives and hearts, which brought me so much joy. I thanked him for Thomas, Marta, Kaisa, Karl, Kenny, Barbara, Paco, Jose, Christian, Sarah, Lisa, David, Charlie, Nacho, Cesar, Stef, Kim, Clara, Marcele, Alba, Marisol, Elena, Oscar, Natalie, Vance, Julie, Dave, Wolfgang, just everyone, and yes, even Neoneé. Perhaps, especially Neoneé. She taught me so much without even trying, without even realizing it. I prayed that someday she would find the joy that believing brings. I will love her unconditionally because I know that she is still a child of my Lord, and I will continue praying that she finds him within her. *Thank you, God, for my crutches and for the angel you sent to deliver them. Please be with him always and let him know how much I appreciate them.* I wiped my tears as I stood up to continue my walk. *Thank you, Lord, for walking with me.*

I gathered my emotional composure as I started back down the sidewalk. I had to figure out a way to get my crutches back home without taking them on the airplane. I knew they would not be allowed as carry-ons. I would ship them home if I had to. I was sure the city of Santiago would have some sort of shipping stores. I'd figure it out when I got there.

> I can do all things through Christ who strengthens me.
> —Philippians 4:13

The closer I got to Santiago, the more difficult it got for me not to cry. I was so overjoyed. I had to find the strength to hold back these tears and keep my composure, as I knew that I would be amongst a crowd fairly soon. Still only a couple miles away, I had encountered only a few pilgrims.

"Buen Camino! Almost there!" we would say to one another as they passed me by.

My gait was still awkward, and I knew I was going to get some unwanted attention with my ambulating struggle. It was actually nice walking this final day, alone 80 percent of the time. It gave me so much more time to spend in prayer with Jesus. As I got closer, sure enough, more and more pilgrims started passing me. I smiled and returned kind greetings. I finally approached the entrance stone with the sign of Santiago de Compostela city limits! I did it! I finally did it! Oh wait, nope, I'm still not there yet. I had to find my way to the cathedral.

Entering Santiago

The shells and signs were super easy to find now. They were practically everywhere. It was very enlightening to start seeing some familiar sights. When I first arrived in Santiago about four weeks ago and spent the night at that first albergue, I didn't realize that I was actually walking on some of the sidewalks that were part of the Camino heading toward the cathedral. The familiar surroundings made me happy, like I was home. It was such a cool feeling. The mall I had visited was right across the street. I passed right by the restaurant I ate at. Super cool!

I kept walking on these ridiculous, something terribly wrong, feet of mine, and with each step even though painful, it was exhilarating! *Is this real? Is this really happening?* I kept putting one foot in front of the other, and even though painful, I was still walking, and that was all that mattered. It was truly miraculous that I was still walking and getting closer and closer to that final destination. *Thank you, Lord. Thank you so very much.*

At last, I saw the first holy cross reaching up above all the buildings, high and mighty, almost caressing the sky. The first cross, a digital extension from the glorious cathedral that houses the remains of St. James, was visible and inviting me to keep placing one foot in front of the other. I was now amongst the hustle and bustle of this busy city. The cobblestone streets, the shoulder-to-shoulder buildings that skyrocketed above me. The smell of fresh bread, croissants, bakeries, and coffee was overwhelming. I edged closer and closer to the site I had spent so much time planning and preparing for. This magical place I just would not let any obstacle prevent me from seeing. And suddenly, as I made that final corner turn, there she stood. It was real. I was here. A tear of joy found its way down my cheek. I felt his presence much more intensely. She was so beautiful, so astonishing, so awe-inspiring. I was full of wonder. I was so amazed.

I had encountered the church from behind and needed to find my way to the front, which I did fairly easily. My crutches carried me to the entrance in the front of the cathedral. The plaza was inundated with exhilarated pilgrims from all walks of life, celebrating their own arrivals. I was a little disappointed that there was construction at the very entrance, thereby not allowing visitors to enter. I had to find the side entrance in order to get inside. The next obstacle was the fact that they wouldn't let you in with a backpack, so I had to go find a locker to temporarily rent, which was close by. The only thing was all this walking back and forth was straining my feet, as if I was adding what felt like an additional hundred miles on my final walking day. Regardless, I was going to make it inside, and at last, I did.

Immediately upon entering the cathedral, my breath was taken away. I could not believe this magnificent sight. It felt like I was in a golden kingdom surrounded by angels protecting its every inch. It was full of people admiring every aspect of this incredible structure. I was completely lost within this religious maze. I was able to find the line that pilgrims and visitors were waiting in to go pay homage to St. James. His remains were laid within a statue made of gold, and anyone who wanted to touch it, caress it, or prayer over it was allowed to for a few seconds, as the line was quite lengthy. There was a sign that clearly stated no photography or videotaping, but I witnessed a gentleman right in front of me doing just that. So I decided I would do the same until someone corrected me. Unfortunately, Jay's GoPro was out of battery.

Suddenly, a familiar face appeared before me. It was Wolfgang! He was just as surprised as I was, and with his huge smile and wide eyes, he yelled out, "Marissa!" I threw my arms around his neck and just started bawling like a baby.

"Oh my goodness, you made it!" he said with great joy.

I, on the other hand, could hardly speak. I was so overcome with joyous emotion. Finally, as I calmed down, I said, "Yes, yes, yes, I made it!" as happy tears continued to roll down my face.

He replied, "I am so thrilled for you. I am so happy to see you here." We settled in a less crowded area in the church and talked quietly. His daughter was at the museum, and he was just taking pictures inside the church. We exchanged contact information so we could try to keep in touch. He told me he had shaved his beard and mustache and cut his hair, so now I knew why he looked a bit younger. He just couldn't get over that I was in this incredible cathedral visiting with him; he was just amazed.

I was so happy that I had made such a good friend with this gentleman and his daughter, even though she was a nonbeliever. I had hope and faith that this experience would answer some questions for her. He was incredibly thankful that she had chosen to do this journey, and he too had hope she would open her mind and her soul just a bit more. I told him that maybe someday I would share all the miracles I experienced on this journey and perhaps that might help someone, anyone, even just one person to question the thought that perhaps God is very real. He was very happy to hear that. We visited awhile longer and then parted ways, promising to keep in touch.

After our visit, I went to retrieve my backpack and stand in line to receive my Compostela. It was a two-hour line by the time I jumped in. I was perfectly fine with that, thinking back on how much I had suffered to get the privilege to stand in this line. Another blessing popped out right in front of me. Right there was the shipping company that would send my crutches home. I asked a friendly couple that was waiting in line behind me if they would save my spot while I tried to ship these special sticks home. They gladly said they would, and I pranced right into the store. There was only one person in front of me, so it didn't take long to get waited on. Once I showed them my crutches, they looked at each other and said they would figure out a way. The young man went to the back to look for a carton or box that they might fit into. In the meantime, the young lady was helping me fill out the forms. Miraculously, everything fell into place, and these two beautiful people made it happen for me. *Thank you, Lord. I simply will never be able to thank you enough for everything that you have done for me. I pray they will arrive to my home safely; they absolutely mean the world to me. How could they not? They are a gift from God himself. There is no doubt in my mind.*

Now, I had to deal with the fact that I would have to walk

around Santiago without them. I was okay with that because I knew I wasn't walking alone. I hadn't walked alone the entire route. They helped me tremendously, and I'm sure I would not have made it to Santiago without their assistance. They had prevented so many falls and had lightened my heavy load.

Once I got back in line, it did not take long to finally approach the desk and the lovely lady who would present to me my earned gift. I had to show her my passport. It was verified, as well as my other documents. She laughed at one of my stamps that I had received from an artist whose stamp was made out of melted wax. He invited pilgrims into his home, which he had converted into a museum infested with all his artwork. He sold whatever he could. He truly was gifted, but I could not carry anything home at that time. I had to prove who I was by showing her my official passport since it had my picture. She was very kind and made friendly conversation. As I was waiting for my Compostela, I admired some cheap bracelets for sale on the counter. I needed to have one to remember this moment. I grabbed a simple brown one with a scallop shell and told her I was purchasing it as I was placing it on my wrist. She smiled and showed me my much-sought-after Compostela. I couldn't even read it because it was written in Latin, but I couldn't stop smiling. I was so very proud of myself. I had to fight back the tears of self-accomplishment. I thanked her kindly and paid her the three euros for the bracelet and left the crowded office area feeling like I was on a cloud. My feet didn't even hurt.

I had decided to go check out Finisterre since the girls were not going to arrive in Santiago until tomorrow afternoon. Therefore, I made a reservation at a hotel in Finisterre and needed to find the bus station to get me there. I had decided on visiting this west coast town because my guidebook instructed me that it was once considered "The End of the World." Apparently, way back yonder, when humankind thought the world was flat, Finisterre was the farthest point on the coast, and one could go no further, thereby acquiring the title, "The End of the World." There is a lighthouse approximately 3.3 km from the city, where the views are breathtaking and the sunsets are unbelievable. I thought to myself, *If it doesn't rain, maybe I will try to get there. I think I can make it another 6.6 km, but that would of course take me triple the time of the average pilgrim, especially without my crutches.* I would try anyway.

I found my way to the tourist office, where I picked up a map. The sweet lady showed me where to find the bus station and said I should look for bus #5, which would get me to the station. By miracle, I got to the corner where it stopped and was the last one to hobble on. I was informed that there was a bus leaving for Finisterre at 2:45 p.m., and that was the one I was shooting for. Unfortunately, once I got to the counter, the young man informed me differently. There was no bus leaving at 2:45 to Finisterre. The next one was not until 7:00. Great, just great. Now I had four hours to kill, and not only that, but most of my day I was planning on spending in that town would vanish by the time I arrived. *It's going to be okay. I'm still going to go, and I will venture around the town tomorrow morning.* There's always more than one solution to every problem.

I settled in a corner in the station and charged my phone and GoPro for about an hour. I started getting hungry, so I went and found a decent restaurant and enjoyed a beverage. I was glad not to be outside during this time because now it was raining super hard. It had been raining practically every day for the past five days, and I was really getting tired of always being wet.

After dinner, I went back to the station and just so happened to engage in a pleasant conversation with a man from Germany. He was relatively young, late twenties, early thirties probably. We shared some of our stories from the Camino. He was getting on a bus to take him back home. He showed me some pictures he had taken of a beach there at Finisterre, and I told him that was where I was hoping to go. I informed him of the challenges my feet were giving me, but by the blessings of my good Lord, my savior Jesus Christ, I had been able to walk up to this day and kept praying that I would be able to enjoy another. He was a believer and said he would also say a prayer for me to continue to Finisterre and enjoy God's blessings. His bus arrived, and he departed, waving a gentle goodbye.

I had two more hours to entertain myself prior to my bus, so I played Candy Crush and messed with Facebook. I had contacted the staff at the hotel where I had made reservations, and they told me they would gladly wait for my arrival, no matter how late I was. So sweet. I love Spain.

Finally, I jumped on the 7:00 bus to Finisterre and napped most of the way. Upon my arrival, I figured out how to get to my hotel. By now, it was just after ten. My feet were hurting, as they did toward the end of the day, but I think I did pretty well, considering I didn't have my crutches. Yes, I wobbled funny, and people looked at me funny, but I was used to it by now. It was still sprinkling, and I had my poncho on. The struggle was that the hotel was two blocks uphill from the station, so naturally I prayed to my Lord to help me make it. He obliged, and I saw the neon sign indicating I had arrived at the right place. *Thank you, God.*

The kind lady checked me in as I was removing my rain jacket. She told me the restaurant stayed open very late, and they would be happy to make me something to eat. I told her I was going to shower, dry up from this drenching rain, and be down later for a quick snack. She handed me the keys, and I found my room.

When I opened the door, I started laughing. I felt like I had just rented a Cinderella room at Walt Disney World. It was a canopy bed with white sachets draped around it. There were lots of pillows and swan-shaped, rolled-up towels inviting me to my bed. It looked like a cross between a rich little girl's room and a honeymoon suite. I couldn't decide. What really took me by surprise was that this little nest was only twenty-five euros. Wow! I love these surprises.

After my shower, I had to figure out a way to dry my poor hiking boots. They had been wet for like five days. My toes were wrinkled every time I took off my boots. So genius me thought creatively and plugged in the blow dryer. I stuck it in my boot and decided to just leave it there to try to dry each one out while I got dressed for dinner.

It worked like magic. Yes, perhaps tomorrow I would get to walk to the lighthouse with dry boots.

I managed to make it downstairs for a snack. I wasn't really hungry for a big meal, so I just ordered some fish soup. I was amazed at how much stuff was in this soup. I thought it was just going to be fish, but it was practically everything that swims in the ocean. It even had octopus in it. I thoroughly enjoyed this seafood delight and thanked the waitress. I was exhausted and needed to get some much-needed rest from this most exciting, spectacular, exhilarating day. *I made it, God. I made it because of you. Thank you, thank you, thank you.* I dried my boots a little bit more, went through my nightly ritual, and zonked out before I could even finish my prayers.

CHAPTER 38

Day 26: September 16th, Finisterre to Santiago

My brethren, count it all joy when you fall into various trials, knowing that the testing of your faith produces patience. But let patience have its complete work, that you may be perfect and complete, lacking nothing.

—James 1:2–4

By this time, I had quit counting my mileage because I figured I had made it to my destination. Truth was I added so many more miles because I could not sit still. I had to walk around to see as much as I could see before I headed back home to Texas. Yes, my feet were still hurting, and I don't know why, but I would figure that out once I got home. For now I wanted to enjoy as much of Spain as I could. Would I ever return to this lovely country? I was not sure; therefore, I would see what my eyes and feet allowed me to, as much of it as I possibly could. I so thoroughly enjoyed every moment there.

I woke up at 7:40 a.m. I couldn't believe it. That was about the latest I had ever slept in, and I truly enjoyed that. I even stayed in bed a little longer and played Candy Crush. I hadn't played since I left home, and I thought about how far Jay was ahead of me by now. We had a competitive thing going on with this silly game and would see who could stay ahead. I thought to myself, *That little twerp. He's probably way ahead of me by now.* Usually I was ahead, but like I said, I hadn't played since I left home, so I stayed in bed and advanced just a few levels. I played until I ran out of lives, which didn't take long. Oh well. I needed to go enjoy this city anyway.

I dried my boots again, even more, although they were fairly dry by now. But what was really nice was when I put them on, they were warm. Oh yes, how good that warm feeling was to my feet. I got dressed, packed up, and checked out. What was really sad though was that it was still raining. My smile turned upside down. It wasn't raining hard, just a drizzle, but enough to put a damper on things and plans for the day. I wasn't going to make it to the beach or the lighthouse. It was gloomy, sprinkling, kind of cold, and just overall dreary. So I decided to venture around this quaint little town and take pictures anyway.

I stopped at a few bars and had a coffee with some breakfast tapas. I went by the harbor and took pictures of the boats. I would catch an early bus back to Santiago and wait for my friends, which I did. I caught my bus and took many pictures of the coast on the way back to Santiago. Perhaps this was best for my feet. I had put them through much turmoil with my undying determination, and this rain was God's way of saying, "Enough is enough." *Okay, Lord, I will listen.*

Upon arrival to Santiago, I decided to splurge and spend one night in a terribly expensive hotel. It was a historical site and hundreds of years old. I tried to reserve a room at Hostal de los Reyes Catolicos, which was a pilgrim's hospital many years ago, converted now to a hotel, but they were out of rooms. So I opted for the historical one behind the cathedral. One hundred euros! Wow, that was a mega splurge for me, and what a disappointment when I opened the door. It was a tiny room, but that was okay. I had the privilege of staying there, and therefore all I could do was smile. It made me realize how fortunate I was to even have enough money to stay there.

I was so terribly fortunate to experience Santiago and its entire splendor. I was fortunate enough to walk into the city with my own two feet. Regardless of the pain I had endured during the pilgrimage, I was fortunate enough to say I made it. And I go back each and every time to give my Lord and my faith in him the credit. Every single step that got me there was due to my belief in him. What I would give to anyone who questioned that. I lay in this historical bed, crying in appreciation for all I had experienced the past four weeks. *How fortunate am I to be his child. Thank you, Lord.*

I unpacked and found myself back at the plaza looking for my friends Marta and Kasia. When I made eye contact with them, they came running up and almost knocked me over! Oh what a joyous feeling to be in my friends' loving embrace!

"Wow! It's Marissa! I can't believe you made it!" both exclaimed.

I was so overwhelmed with their presence and their loving embrace I just couldn't help but allow the tears of joy to flow. We jumped up and down and just kept hugging and hugging each other like we were long-lost cousins. I was more or less jumping with my knees up and down, not my feet, for I dared not brutalize them anymore. It was such a great experience. I wish all of the world could do this with people you know for a few hours.

We laughed and talked and eventually made our way into the cathedral for their first viewing. I had to inform them of the no-backpack rule. We checked them in and returned to the church. They were just as bewildered as I was the first time I saw the inside of this magical kingdom. We made plans for dinner and met later that evening with about twenty of our pilgrim friends we all had made along the way.

> Therefore, as the elect of God, holy and beloved, put on tender mercies, kindness, humility, meekness, longsuffering; bearing with one another, and

forgiving one another, if anyone has a complaint against another; even as Christ forgave you, so you also must do. But above all these things put on love, which is the bond of perfection.

—Colossians 3:12–14

Dinner was such a blast. We ate, we drank, laughed, and shared our stories. I thought to myself, *What would happen if we took the leaders of this world and they all went on a pilgrimage?* Walking with God changes the way you think about things. You look at your fellow man in a deeper, more caring sense. That is what this world needs. At the end of their travels, these leaders would all come together and have dinner just as we were having right now. How easy it would be to solve so many world problems. How simple it would be to come together as one world family. How wonderful it would be to become one world where differences were respected. Oh what a wonderful thought.

It reminded me of John Lennon's song "Imagine." Although in his song he mentions, "Imagine there's no countries, It isn't hard to do, Nothing to live or die for and no religion too." Religion is a necessary factor in our world because that is what keeps people on the righteous path. It teaches us his holy Word. Some people need religion more than others. I believe religion is essential and good, but being spiritual is just a bit different. One can be religious without being spiritual. That is not a good. Tonight I was sitting with many different religions and perhaps one or two who didn't even believe, but that was okay. I knew God still loved them. I would seek a way to perhaps plant a seed in their future to think about it. Dinner was with so many corners of the world, and I was so privileged to be a part of it. Best of all, God was sitting at our table.

After such a beautiful evening with my friends, I found my way and limped back to my room. I spent the rest of the evening in reflection of this entire experience and fell asleep after my routine. I thanked all my Facebook followers for continuously sending their endless prayers. I was so fortunate that I had prayer armies rooting for me the entire time. My cousin Maricela and my sister-in-law, Sylvia, were the prayer warriors that took charge and reassured me they would not stop until I made it home. I love them dearly. Thank you, my gracious Lord.

CHAPTER 39

Thursday: September 17th, Santiago to the Albergue

Be kindly affectionate to one another with brotherly love, in honor giving preference to one another; not lagging in diligence, fervent in spirit, serving the Lord;

—Romans 12:10–11

Today, I would spend some time at the pilgrims' mass at the cathedral, shop for trinkets for my loved ones, and find my way to the last and final albergue. I so thoroughly enjoyed this day. I ran into many of my friends, I got my nails done, I shopped around, and I visited the church one last time before I got on the bus to take me back to the very first albergue I spent the night at. It would also be my last albergue. How coincidental is that? I paid my dues, found my bunk, and this time it was the lower one! Yes! It wasn't quite as crowded this time, perhaps because now it was September, and the number of pilgrims may be lower this time of year. I showered, reflected, Facebooked, and prayed. I am so very thankful that we have such a giving God, such a loving God. I have never felt so much happiness, so much appreciation, so much love, ever in my life. I have grown closer to my Lord, and I find it so intriguing that this was not my original plan.

Just as my friend Christina once told me, "If you want to make God laugh, tell him you have a plan."

I fell asleep in the deepest depths of happiness anyone could ever ask for.

CHAPTER 40

Friday: September 18th, Santiago to Corpus Christi

Love suffers long and is kind; love does no envy; love does not parade itself, is not puffed up; does not behave rudely, does not seek its own, is not provoked, thinks no evil; does not rejoice in iniquity, but rejoices in the truth; bears all things, believes all things, hopes all things, endures all things.

—Corinthians 13:4–7

I was going home. I had never appreciated family or home more than I did the previous few weeks. I wanted nothing more than to see my family, my children, my mom, my boyfriend, my sister, my aunt, my brother and sister-in-law, my nephews and niece. All I wanted was my family. My loved ones. I learned over the previous four weeks how important my loved ones were to me. I wanted nothing more than to see the most important people in my life waiting for me at the airport.

My flight was lengthy, as expected. All I did the entire time was pray and pray and pray. I thanked God for all he had done for me, especially carrying me to Santiago. I truly felt that it was my faith, just as Jay had brought to my attention several weeks before when I first started having trouble walking; it was my faith that was being tested. He told me, "It's either your determination or your faith," and he said he leaned toward my faith. My faith was being tested, and I dwelled on that thought. I know for a fact that the only reason I was able to walk into the city of Santiago is because God made it happen. He sent me so many angels, so many miracles, so many signs and feelings and directions. God talked to me, silently in his own special and meaningful ways, and God spoke to me through actions of others. Not in a humanist fashion, such as voices; God spoke to me in a spiritual sense. Only if you believe can you hear him. Inside, he tells you what is right, what is good, what is just. God exists in all of us if you just listen spiritually. I know he is real because he saved me, because he answered my prayers, because he walked with me, because he carried me.

It was after seven at night when the plane touched down in Corpus Christi, Texas. How bizarre is that? I live in a city that in translation means "The Body of Christ." All I wanted was for my entire family, the people I love the most, to be present at the airport. I missed them all so much and needed to be in their arms. I wanted to run up to Jay and wrap my arms around him, which is exactly what happened when I arrived.

I could not control my tears of joy. My mom and sister Thelma were there. My daughters, Nikki, Gina, and Laura, made it complete. I love them all so dearly; they are my world. My brother, sister-in-law, and nephews, along with several other family members were all waiting for me at a restaurant in downtown Corpus. It could not have been more perfect.

Upon arrival at the restaurant, we had the entire patio closed off for this special homecoming occasion. Margaritas had been ordered, chips and salsa were waiting for me on the table, and the hugs and kisses lasted for quite some time until I got enough love from each and every family member present. My only sibling unable to make it was Jaime, because he lives in Maryland. I spoke to him as well. I handed out gifts to everyone, and then I made the girls and my nephews put on the shirts I had bought them. We then took several pictures and toasted to commemorate my safe homecoming on this lovely evening. Everyone, especially Jay and my sister, were worried about my feet since I was still walking funny and still having some pain. I promised I would go visit my podiatrist on Monday morning. For now though, all I wanted to do was spend time with my beautiful, loving family. My homecoming was more than I could have asked for. *Thank you, Lord, for bringing me home. Thank you, Lord, for being my home.*

Jay drove me to the condo, and we caught up on just being in each other's arms and presence. He is such a beautiful person. He even looked prettier to me now that I was home!

We talked a lot until he put his finger on my lips and said, "Go to sleep, love. We have tomorrow."

I smiled and closed my eyes. *I love you, baby.*

PART III

The Finale

CHAPTER 41

Monday: September 21st, The Final Diagnosis

That you may walk worthy of the Lord, fully pleasing Him, being fruitful in every good work and increasing in the knowledge of God; strengthened with all might, according to his glorious power, for all patience and long-suffering with joy; giving thanks to the Father, who has qualified us to be partakers of the inheritance of the saints in the light.

—Colossians 1:10–12

Jay waited on me hand and foot the entire weekend. He knew I was still in pain, and my feet would swell easily if I was up on them too much. I wasn't wearing my boots anymore, and shoes were just terribly uncomfortable. Monday morning was finally here. I had to do something to correct my inability to walk and curve some of this pain before I had to return to work on the following Wednesday. I just couldn't imagine having to be on my feet for twelve hours, especially up and down those long hallways in the hospital. Remember, I am a nurse, and sitting down just because your feet hurt is not an option. I was anxious about having to return to work in that condition.

We arrived at Dr. Aeby's office exactly at 9:00 a.m. I had called last Friday during one of my layovers, informing them I would be there to figure this dilemma out, so they were expecting me. I had talked to them twice while I was in Spain, letting them know what was going on, so they were familiar with my case. When he called me back to the exam room, he assessed everything he needed to. He then asked me to take a walk down the hall as he observed my gait. It appeared to be the classic plantar fasciitis. All of my symptoms were classic fasciitis. His thorough assessment again pointed to fasciitis. There was no reason to believe otherwise. He said I should take another week off, recommended certain shoes, and wrote me a prescription. I still couldn't imagine being pain-free in a week.

Then I remembered he had x-rayed my feet last year due to some issues I was experiencing at work. My best friend, Susan, the other core charge nurse, recommended him, as she had the same issues. He did an awesome job taking care of both Susan and me back then. So I asked him if we could do a comparison x-ray. He thought that was a splendid idea and followed through. I wobbled over to the room where he had his machine, and he x-rayed each foot. I made it back to the exam room and waited with Jay for Dr. Aeby's return.

A few minutes later, when he walked back into the room, Dr. Aeby just shook his head and said, "This changes everything."

What? I didn't know exactly what he meant, nor did Jay, until he posted both x-rays up on the viewing screen and turned the light on.

He then informed us as he was staring at the x-rays, "You have 100 percent complete stress fractures across both of your calcaneus bones, your heels." He pointed with his pencil, showing the thick white lines down both of my heel bones. "You've basically been walking on broken feet! By the appearance of the fractures, it looks like you've had this injury for approximately three weeks. Your left heel is a more jagged line, which is probably more painful. See the difference as compared to your right heel, which is a fine straight line?"

Now it all made sense to me. It was exactly three weeks ago when the imaginary yet very real knives went through both of my feet. The scenario of silently screaming as I plopped back down in my bunk ran through my head. *Oh my goodness, I've been walking on broken feet!* I was speechless.

Dr. Aeby then looked at me and questioned, "And you walked several hundred miles, huh? How did you do that?"

At that moment, Jay and I looked at each other. I then turned back to Dr. Aeby and honestly responded with, "I was carried."

CHAPTER 42

My Journey's Conclusion

> Yet for us there is one God, the Father, from whom are
> all things and for whom we exist, and one Lord, Jesus
> Christ, through whom are all things and through whom
> we live.
>
> —1 Corinthians 8:6

Jason, my director, was not very happy that I had to take the next five weeks off of work and take a short-term leave of absence in order to allow my heels to heal properly. I was instructed to stay off of them completely, and if it was absolutely necessary to get out of bed, I needed to wear high heels. That would put all my weight on the balls of my feet.

But I had to go fishing. Do you know how difficult it is to walk on the beach with high heels? I was going to have to figure out a way to still participate in Sharkathon, which was just a couple of weeks away, with my broken feet. I was sure I could figure it out. Jay was an absolute angel and the best private-duty nurse I could ever have asked for. He saw to it that I did not miss the tournament. *Thank you, Lord, for this blessing.*

Sharing my story was something I believe my pastor, David, was telling me to do in his message regarding purpose. It was during one of his sermons that he said everyone has a purpose in their life, and finding it is the challenge. "God has a plan for you," he told us. I thought to myself, *I have to share my journey with more than the people who followed me on Facebook. I have to share it with anyone who would be interested in reading these simple words that collectively hold a powerful message.* God is real. Someone out there who does not believe or just isn't sure might ponder on the thought that perhaps he is, according to my testimony. For I have been tried and tested. I am not counterfeit. God is very real, and it was he who picked me up and carried me on that initial devastating day and every day thereafter. My faith in him grew astronomically throughout my journey. I found him inside of me. I found him in other people, in friends and strangers alike. I believe he is the good that exists in all of us, whether you believe in him or not.

Anyone who does not love does not know God, because God is love.

—1 John 4:8

God is good; good is God. Would it be helpful to exchange the word to better understand who he is? Everything in our world, everything in our lives that is good, that is God. I see him in the beauty that his creation possesses. The kindness we show to one another, the love we share with each other, the generosity we give, all of this is God. The good deeds we go out of our way to accomplish, the happiness we see in our children's eyes, the joy we experience during holidays or special occasions, that is God. When you've done something good and you feel good about yourself, that is the existence of God inside of you. "Here, let me help you," or, "Oh no, you go ahead." That is God. Caring is God. Loving is God. A simple concept if you believe in good. A much more complicated one if you can't understand something that simple. A time of darkness is the absence of God, and that is when you need him the most. For if you believe, he will carry you too.

> For God so loved the world, that He gave His only begotten Son, that whoever believes in Him should not perish but have eternal life. For God did not send his Son into the world to condemn the world, but that the world through Him might be saved.
>
> —John 3:16–17

REFERENCES

The Holy Bible, The New King James Version.
Copyright 1988 Thomas Nelson, Inc.

The Northern Caminos, The Norte, Primitivo and Inglés Routes by
Dave Whitson and Laura Perazzoli. Cicerone, first edition 2012,
second edition 2015.